Greg and Felicity's
History of Magic

By
Greg Chapman

First paperback edition 2023

www.gregandfelicity.com

THIS BOOK IS DEDICATED

TO

PAMELA AND SHAZU

TWO INCREDIBLE LADIES
WHO TOUCHED OUR LIVES
WITH THEIR OWN SPECIAL
MAGIC.

Contents

Cosmic Xposure

Overture

A few days ago, when I began my work on this book, I was asked an interesting question while performing close-up magic for some teachers in High Wycombe.

"Is magic real?" asked one of the teachers sitting around the table onto which I had just deposited a deck of cards. I found this a complicated moment to be asked this question, as, for me, a deck of cards holds within it a fundamental suggestion of trickery and cheating rather than of 'real magic'.

As I say to my audiences during some performances, "Imagine you wake up with real magical powers tomorrow morning. Think of all the things you could do with magic. Then think about how far down the list of uses of your magical powers you would be before you started asking strangers to 'pick a card'."

It is up to the magician performing a card trick to transcend this first impression (if they choose).

I try very hard to leave my audiences with no false impressions of me and who I am. I try to be, as a biography of 'The Amazing Randy' was titled, an 'honest liar'. I want them to know that I am using skill, deception, knowledge of people, and good old-fashioned trickery to give the appearance of magical effects happening. Yet, at the same time, I want to leave them, through the presentation of these effects, the stories I wrap them in, with a sense of wonder and, in the truest sense of the word, 'magic'.

So how do I answer the question when asked straight out when the card deck hits the table?

To answer in the affirmative and to suggest that I am a wizard who uses his extraordinary powers to entertain at a Christmas party instead of solving the significant problems of the world would seem both dishonest and slightly absurd (and not in the way I like to be somewhat absurd in my performance on occasion). However, an answer in the negative would not only suck some of the energy and some of the wonder from the table, but it would also not be entirely accurate to my thoughts about magic, that it is a feeling, an idea, a moment of wonder.

I looked past the dinner plates containing traces of brussels sprouts and gravy directly into the eyes of the teacher who had asked the question.

"Magic is real," I told her. "Magic is finding somebody who loves and cares for you as much as you do them and sharing many moments of wonder."

There was silence at the table as everyone processed these words.

"You're a romantic!" she told me, slightly accusingly, with a laugh. I laughed, nodded in acknowledgement, and proceeded to take the cards out of the box and continue with the trick.

If I am to answer the accusation of being a bit of a romantic in that situation, then I have to say I'm guilty as charged. It would be hard to argue otherwise when you see both my name and my wife's in the title of this book and on the title of the documentary we will be creating alongside it (also titled 'Greg and Felicity's History of Magic', in case you should want to find it online)[1]. I am, however, something of a combination of a romantic and something of a realist, a stoic combined with an optimist.

I can, therefore, quite comfortably tell you that all of the magic which you see me perform is nothing more than a series of tricks while at the same time hoping that you can still take wonder, joy, and perhaps even your own moment

---

[1] For details of where 'Greg and Felicity's History of Magic' and our other documentaries can be watched, visit www.gregandfelicity.com).

of magic from the simple effects which I perform, and some which may even last you well after I have performed for you. For me, that is the essence of a magician's art.

This is the magic that this book deals with. It is not a history concerning the wizards and magic of legends or of 'witchcraft' (except where witchcraft and magic tricks cross paths), but a history of the art of magic, and the joy of magic, seen through the eyes of someone who is both a performer of magic and also a magic fan.

If you are looking for a dry, academic tome on the history of magic, this is not it.

This book will take in the history of magic and the wonder of magic. It will mix historical facts with my thoughts, opinions, philosophies, and musings. However, unlike when performing a magic trick, I will attempt to delineate between what is definitively true and where I am leading you down pathways of wonder and speculation. The book is aimed at magic fans, those interested in history, and perhaps even my fellow magicians to enjoy. Whether or not I succeed will ultimately be for you, my dear reader, to decide.

This book does not claim to be a 'complete history of magic' – such a task would be nearly impossible, and I can almost guarantee that had I attempted such a feat, I would be chastised on release for the people and tricks I had left out[2].

I have arranged this book in vaguely chronological order, although some chapters will bounce around time a little more when I look at certain subjects.

As a personal history of magic, you will also find that this book focuses mainly on the 'Western' traditions and history of magic and the history leading towards the world of magic which I inhabit, having spent my performance career so far mainly in Europe.

One final note before I finish this overture and raise the curtain on my main performance, and that is a word on the authorship of this book. If you are astute, you will note that there are two names listed atop the front of this book, Greg and Felicity, and you may wonder where the mysterious Felicity is hiding during the course of this introduction and through the book's text. Is she, perhaps, an assistant, tucked away in some hidden compartment about to burst forth in a flash of light and a puff of smoke at the wave of this magician's wand?

No, she is not. I may get onto my personal feelings and philosophy about 'magicians' assistants' later in the book, but for now, I will clarify that Felicity is nobody's assistant. As documentary makers, we are equals, co-

---

[2] Although I fear this is likely, as, especially in sections covering the last couple of hundred years I have had to be selective, and I know I have left some big names out.

presenters, and co-creators of all we do. In magic, however, things are a bit different.

Felicity is one of the most important people that a magician can ever have in their life, somebody who enjoys watching the magic, with no wish to know how it is done, and who cares enough about the magician to give them honest feedback and direction from the point of view of the audience. Countless are the times she has pointed out odd movements I am making on stage, which often appear to give away the trick's method. This is crucial, as whether these movements point to the way the trick is done or would seem to indicate a method which I am, in fact, not using, the result is still to take away the feeling of magic in the audience.

Felicity has provided the same service throughout the creation of this book, as I have shared stories with her while I have been researching the book, and her reaction to different stories has helped me to know which of the stories will be of greater or lesser interest to people who are outside of the world of magic.

You may not notice Felicity's presence, but rest assured she is there backstage, and her presence has been felt on every page of this book.

Thank you all for joining us on a journey into the history of magic and allowing me to guide you through the subject.

Cosmic Xposure

Terms of Art

Before we begin, I should share some terms used in the book. I have heard all of these terms used by different magicians and magic fans, and many of them seem to have a different perspective of what each of these words mean, particularly with confusion between the words 'trick' and 'effect'.

Therefore, what follows are my definitions of these words, which some magicians (and magicians I very much respect) may well disagree with. I do not hold these up as the *correct* definitions of these words. However, they are the meaning of these words as long as I use them within the four corners of the pages of this book. Please do not write to me to tell me that you disagree with my definitions – in the real world, I will bow down to any definition you wish to place on these words – but between the covers of this book (or within the kilobytes of data it takes up on your eBook reader), my words, or rather the way I choose to define my words, is as follows:

Trick – The basic building block of magic. The trick is what the audience sees, stripped bare of any context or story surrounding it. The trick is clever, but it lacks depth and, on its own, is designed purely to fool the audience, not to entertain them. *Simple example: I ask you to pick a card. You take the card and look at it. I tell you what the card is.*

Effect – As you can see from above, a trick may present a puzzle – how did I know what your card was? This, however, is an unsatisfactory performance as it offers nothing more than a puzzle; it doesn't have any depth. The effect is the 'story' and performance that the magician builds around the trick to make it more interesting. *Simple example: I take out an old deck of cards, place them on the table, and talk about an old magician I met once, living on the streets of Turin, Italy. He had a deck of cards, the very deck of cards that is now on the table, and he would offer passing people the chance to pick a card, to look at it, but not to let him see it (at this point, I offer the cards to someone to choose one). I then tell them that the old magician would look deep into the person's eyes as though he could see the thoughts moving in their minds (I would now look deep into the person's eyes). I never understood how he did it, but a smile would come across his face as he stared. He would tell them he could see so many happy thoughts hiding away in their minds but that the most recent thought was of hearts dancing around. Three hearts, to be exact. At this point, I would ask the person to turn their card over and reveal the three of hearts.*

Method – The method is very simply how the trick is achieved, the 'secret' that the magician never reveals to the member of the public. This is very subtly different from the 'trick', for the same 'trick' could be performed using various methods, and indeed some of the best 'effects' involve repetitions of the same 'trick' using multiple different 'methods'. *Simple example: Let us consider the trick outlined above. Perhaps the most straightforward method for achieving this would be with a deck of cards that were all the same. Therefore there would only be one card you could choose.*

Magician – Somebody who performs magical effects. For me, it is not enough to know a trick to be a magician. You must perform the trick as an effect to bring joy, wonder, or magic to someone. You do not, however, have to be highly skilled, a 'professional', or a member of any club, circle, or society to be a magician. You have to perform magic. Please note that I would not include in this category anybody who uses magic to cheat, con, or mislead people for nefarious reasons.

Camera Trick – Filmmaking, not magic.

Participant – An audience member who is directly involved in a specific effect. The most obvious example would be somebody picking a card in a card trick, although this can expand to include everyone present. For example, in some of my shows, some effects involve every member of the audience making choices or even handling or checking props themselves.

Audience – The people watching the effect who are not participants. They are still 'involved' in the effect in an emotional and attentive capacity (or should be, in my opinion), but they are not directly participating or influencing the flow of the whole effect.

In The Beginning...

As with most things in history, the further back in time you go with the history of magic, the murkier things become, and the harder it is to separate fact from speculation, and the less information and evidence remains.

This doesn't just happen with the history of magic but also with the performance of many of the magical effects I perform. By the time I reach the end of many of my effects, I hope that, through how I structure the effect, you may have forgotten or misremembered some of the earlier steps. This isn't always necessary. Otherwise, the magic tricks performed in the documentary linked to this book would be far too easy to figure out on a second viewing. However, it is still a valuable tool for a magician to be able to slightly blur the past within an effect to enhance the trick.

With history, however, it is incredibly unhelpful when you reach a point where the past can no longer be seen clearly or, for that matter, be seen at all. We will never know the name of the first magician to perform a simple magic trick or even whether the first magic trick may have even been before the concept of names existed.

For the record, we are well into the area of speculation here.

How many of us have, for example, while out playing 'Fetch' with a dog, pretended to throw the ball while secretly hiding the ball behind our back in the other hand? If you never have, I can strongly recommend it, provided you have a dog with a good temperament who won't respond to such a trick by, for example, after getting the ball, dropping it into the sea and coming back to shore so that you have to get soaking wet trying to get it back, while the dog in question sits on the beach and enjoys getting the last laugh. Not, of course, that I speak from experience.

If you have ever done this and seen your dog disappearing into the distance to chase an imaginary ball, then I'm sure you can imagine that someone in the past may have done the same, not to a pet, but to someone of their own species.

Although it is still unclear when our ancestors started using tools, as new evidence still comes to light which may push the date further into the past, we can be pretty sure that two point six million years ago, some of the Homo habilis who were alive at the time were using tools. How much of a stretch of the imagination does it take to believe that in more than six point five million years from the first tools to the first cave paintings, some early ancestor, somewhere, convinced his fellows that he could make objects disappear by throwing them into the air in the same way that we might do for our pets today?

That, however, is in the realm of prehistory, which is outside the remit of this book, and so begins the difficult task of trying to pin down the first recorded magician, or at the very least, the first recorded magic trick in history – and in this, we will not count descriptions of 'magic' where it is unclear whether these are recounting a trick, or mythical or legendary acts with supernatural powers being assumed, such as Moses parting the Red Sea in Biblical tales.

For some years, I was under the misapprehension that the first recorded magic trick came in the form of wall art in the Ancient Egyptian tomb at Beni Hasan because I had read this in several accounts of the history of magic.

The story of the tomb at Beni Hasan begins in Egypt, near the banks of the River Nile, where a cemetery was built over a period of years from the later part of the Old Kingdom of Ancient Egypt (c. 2345-2181 BC), through the First Intermediate Period (c. 2181-2055BC), and into the Middle Kingdom (c. 2055-1650BC).

Were the picture on the tomb wall genuinely to be an image showing a magician performing the cups and balls, it would be an incredible piece of the history of magic. So having heard about it, I was expecting to see something awe-inspiring, whereas what I actually saw the first time I saw an image showing what the artwork on the tomb wall looked like, it was something like this:

Quite clearly, this is not the cups and balls magic trick unless the balls have flat bases, are as big as the cups, and the magicians are performing the same trick for each other. In fact, this is likely an image showing the preparation of foodstuff, quite possibly some form of bread.

Even though the suggestion that we have evidence of the cups and balls in Ancient Egypt is erroneous, this is a stretching of the truth but doesn't change the fact that the oldest confirmed magic trick really is the cups and balls, and while it is not as old as the tombs at Beni Hassan, we can trace it back two thousand years to the First Century AD.

Seneca the Younger was a Stoic Philosopher[3] who lived in Ancient Rome, tutored the young Emperor Nero, and became his advisor. Sadly, he didn't maintain his influence over Nero and eventually committed suicide in 65AD on Emperor Nero's orders after he was accused (probably falsely) of being involved in a plot to assassinate the emperor.

Our interest in Seneca, for the purposes of this book at least, is contained in a series of letters he wrote in the last few years of his life, the 'Epistulae Morales ad Lucilium' ('Moral Letters to Lucilius') and specifically to letter 45, and to one sentence in particular when he is discussing wordplay used to make arguments.

The crucial sentence, written in around 62AD, is:

"Such quibbles are just as harmlessly deceptive as the juggler's cups and dice[4], in which it is the very trickery that pleases me."

This first description of a magic trick has a couple of interesting points to it. The first is that jugglers and magicians are conflated in this description, and indeed, these arts often go together well, requiring a degree of dexterity. Later in the book, we will learn about the 19th

---

[3] Stoic Philosophy is an interesting subject, well outside the remit of this book. If you want to find out more about the subject, and about Seneca, while also being interested in the thoughts of magicians, then I can highly recommend the book '*Happy*' by Derren Brown.

[4] In alternative translations I have seen this translated as 'pebbles' rather than 'dice', although I fear my very rudimentary Latin is not up to reading Seneca in the original Latin.

Century magician Jean Eugine Robert-Houdin, also a juggler. In Las Vegas today you can see Penn Jillette in the Penn & Teller Show, also a juggler and magician, and I fit myself into this enduring tradition, as I learned juggling long before magic became my career.

The references to juggling and trickery also make it very clear that in this earliest recorded trick, it was well known that skill and manipulation were being used to achieve the appearance of magic, which we will learn later in the book is not always the case, and that even today there are people prepared to use magic tricks to claim supernatural powers.

What I find most interesting about this line is how short it is and what a throwaway comment this mention of the trick is. Seneca makes no effort to describe or clarify what he means, implying that he assumed that the recipient, Lucilius, would be familiar with the trick, even though he lives not in Rome but in Sicily. This suggests that at that point in time, the trick was relatively commonplace and would be instantly recognisable.

For a slightly more detailed description of the trick, we have to move forward in time to more letters, written as fictional letters by a writer from approximately the Third Century AD by the name of Alciphron. In the second volume of the letters, one supposedly sent from Napaeus to Creniades, we find a reaction to seeing a magician perform.

"I remember one thing, which struck me dumb with astonishment. A man came forward with a three-legged

table. On this, he placed three little cups, under which he hid some little round white pebbles, such as we find on the bank of a torrent. At one time he put them separately, one under each cup; at another time he showed them, all together, under one cup; then he made them disappear from the cups, I don't know how, and showed them, the next moment, in his mouth. After this he swallowed them, called some of the spectators on to the platform, and pulled out of their nose, head, and ears the pebbles which he ended by juggling away altogether. What a clever thief the man must be, far sharper than Eurybates of Oechalia, of whom we have often heard. I am sure I don't want to see him in the country; since nobody would be able to catch him in the act, he would plunder the house without being noticed.”

I find this description remarkable, not only in the fact that it reflects the 'astonishment' upon seeing the cups and balls (an astonishment which I have felt watching cup and ball routines and have seen on the faces of my audiences) but also because it is so familiar and talks about elements of the trick which you will see performed in many variations of the trick today.

I also find it interesting that in writing this, Alciphron makes the leap from watching a magician to worrying about the magician using their abilities for dishonest reasons. Although it is said in fun, many times, when I approach a table at a close-up performance, someone (always male so far) warns everyone to keep an eye on their wallets as 'the magician' is about.

It appears that, from one of the earliest descriptions of a magic trick right through to the present day, people have always formed a link between magicians and thieves, pickpockets and other crimes. I can safely say that I have never studied pickpocketing or used my magic skills to get away with a crime. I have, however, used my escapology training to help friends a few times who have locked themselves out or lost a key to a padlock, and they are often a little unnerved by how quickly many locks can be opened without needing a key.

Since the description of the trick that we find in the works of Seneca and Alciphron, there have been countless variations of the cup and ball trick and deviations from the basic format of the trick. Some magicians still use three cups, while others now use a single cup. Pebbles and dice have evolved into balls, fruit and other small objects.

The range of cups being used is huge - sometimes there are wooden cups, metal cups, intricately carved or deliberately left plain. I have just started performing my cup and ball routine with paper coffee cups, whereas you can see Penn and Teller performing their version with clear plastic cups[5]. In 1978, King Charles III (when he was Prince Charles) got in on the action when he performed the 'Cups and Balls' as an audition for the Magic Circle[6].

---

[5] I strongly recommend that you take a look at Penn and Teller's version with the three cups, and then treat yourself to Paul Daniels performing his cup and ball, which for me is the absolute pinnacle of the effect.

[6] One common question I am asked when performing is whether I am a member of the Magic Circle, and my answer is 'No'. I don't have anything against the Magic

This is where the separation between trick and effect, which I discussed in the 'Terms of Art' at the start of this book, becomes so important. You can see a hundred people performing tricks with cups and balls, and indeed, most magic sets I have seen include a version of the trick.

What really shows the power of magic, and the inventiveness of good magicians, is the number of different variations and stories which people have come up with over the years. That is why I will never tire of watching a skilled magician performing a trick which has been entertaining people for two millennia.

Circle, and if you are interested in magic then I certainly encourage you to investigate it further to see if it is for you.

My reason for not joining is a simple one. As I understand it (and a quick look at the rules suggests this still to be true), on joining the Magic Circle the magician must promise not to disclose any magic secrets, or methods, except to a genuine student of magic.

This is not a promise I could make in good faith.

I have a couple of magic tricks which I will specifically teach to someone at a show or close-up performance who shows an interest in magic, and who I think will gain some joy from, or share some joy with, that trick.

I will also, later in this very book, be sharing a couple of magic secrets, whether you are a genuine student of magic or not. These secrets may be hundreds of years old, and readily available in print, but were I a member of the magic circle who had made that promise, I would still consider this to be breaking my word.

Cosmic Xposure

The Dark Ages Of Magic

Before I get complaints from historians, I am aware that
the title 'The Dark Ages' is no longer in widespread use
amongst historians, mainly because it underestimates the
period of time from the fall of the Roman Empire to the
Renaissance, lumping it together as a period where
knowledge and understanding of the world was seen to
have taken a step backwards, in contrast with the
'enlightened' times of the Roman Empire and from the
Renaissance onwards. It also points to a shortage of
information about the time. Medieval historians often
argue that both statements undersell this period from the
past.

However, when it comes to the art of magic, this term may be slightly more accurate to a discussion of the period from around 400AD to around 1500AD, as there is little information about what was happening with the art of magic throughout this period. This may partly be because people weren't keeping records of magical performances throughout this period, but also because, with the rise of Christianity throughout Europe, performances of magic could easily be confused with other forms of 'magic', including spells, charms, and healing, in any ways which were contrary to the teachings of The Church.

I use the term 'The Church' here because a combination of low literacy rates, along with failure to translate the Bible into languages which most people could understand even if they could read, meant that the flow of information about religion and what people needed to do to win their place in heaven, was controlled by the member of The Church who spread the 'Word of God' in this era[7].

It was Augustine of Hippo, later to become Saint Augustine, who gives us our first record of a 'Christian' view on magic following the time when Emperor

---

[7] It is also interesting that, certainly at the start of this era, people didn't read in their heads. As you are reading this book, you are most likely not speaking the words aloud. How strange this would have been to a person at the start of the Dark Ages is shown in a passage from St Augustine's Confessions (written 397-400AD), in which he wrote about the Bishop of Milan:
"But when Ambrose used to read, his eyes were drawn through the pages, while his heart searched for its meaning; however, his voice and tongue were quiet. Often when we were present (for anyone could approach him and it was not his habit that visitors be announced to him) we saw him reading in this fashion, silently and never otherwise."

Constantine gave religion an official status in 337AD, less than two decades before Augustine's birth.

In this period, as Christianity was still developing and taking shape, many Christian theologians of the time were still working towards an agreed 'canon' of ideas and philosophies which would form the basis of the religion, and during Augustine's life, there were still conflicts over which books belonged within The Bible[8], and indeed with some differing denominations, these disagreements over both doctrine and books continue to this day.

In Augustine's view, magic (and he specifically uses the Latin term 'Magia') came to people through the power of demons working for Lucifer, the Devil himself.

The extract below is from Augustine's 'City of God', Book 21, Chapter 6:

"And that men may provide these attractions, the devils first of all cunningly seduce them, either by imbuing their hearts with a secret poison, or by revealing themselves under a friendly guise, and thus make a few of them their disciples, who become the instructors of the multitude. For unless they first instructed men, it was impossible to know what each of them desires, what they shrink from, by what

---

[8] A few years ago, while in Turkey filming one of our documentaries, '*Turkey: Fairy Chimneys and Underground Cities*', we learned that the Council of Laodicea in 363AD chose not to include the Book of Revelations as a canonical book of The Bible. I am quite sure this was for strictly theological reasons, and not because that in a letter to the Church of Laodicea it describes them as *"wretched, pitiful, poor, blind and naked"*.

name they should be invoked or constrained to be present. Hence the origin of magic and magicians."

This is very much talking of supernatural 'magic' performed by the demons, which of course, he considered entirely different from the 'miracles' performed by God through Jesus and the Saints.

However, if Seneca and Alciphron before Augustine had made it clear that there was an understanding that some magicians or jugglers performed magical effects using natural means and sleight of hand, then surely Augustine would be happy with these performers as they were not in league with Satan?

Sadly not.

Augustine goes on to describe a potential working method of a trick whereby *"two magnets have been adjusted, one in the roof, another in the floor, so that an iron image is suspended in mid-air between them, one would suppose by the power of the divinity, were he ignorant of the magnets above and beneath"*.

He then discusses a temple to Venus where an inextinguishable lamp would point to that goddess performing what would, I assume, have been considered a miracle if it were related to Augustine's God. As it was in the temple of a pagan god, however, Augustine is willing to accept either demons or man are involved in this effect:

"That lamp, therefore, was either by some mechanical and human device fitted with asbestos, or it was arranged by magical art in order that the worshippers might be astonished, or some devil under the name of Venus so signally manifested himself that this prodigy both began and became permanent."

Augustine then goes on to make an argument, using a form of circular logic which I have no doubt Seneca would have spotted and once again compared to the tricks of the 'juggler's cups and dice', to conclude that any demonstration of magic displayed outside of the work of the Christian God must either be a demon leading a person astray and providing them with magical powers, or a person using natural means to pretend to produce magical effects, in which case *"by the help of magicians, whom Scripture calls sorcerers and enchanters, the devils could gain such power"*. He also specifically goes on to reference a line from Virgil about a woman whose *"charms can cure what souls she please"*.

This work by Augustine, and others like him, are the reasons why, as Christianity spread across Europe and beyond in what I am referring to as the 'Dark Ages', the art of Magic lost prominence, and, although we can be sure it continued as we see the line of the cups and balls throughout history, we lack records of their performance, and have to rely on evidence that is little and far between in order to confirm that magicians continued to perform their tricks throughout this time.

In 1159AD, John of Salisbury, who apparently used to refer to himself as Johannes Parvus, or John the Little, but was not, to the best of my knowledge, a friend of Robin Hood, published his 'De nugis curialium et uestigiis philosophoru' ('On the Frivolities of Courtiers and the Footprints of Philosophers'), in which the first book is devoted to 'Hunting, Theatre[9] and Magic'.

In his chapter on magic he discusses many different forms which magic can take, from divination of the future, to controlling people through making figures and all sorts of other forms. However, he also refers explicitly to 'Praestigium', a word commonly used to mean an illusion, or to confuse someone, suggesting he had knowledge that some of the magic he was discussing was nothing more than a trick. Indeed, the word 'prestidigitation' would go on to become a term for conjuring tricks or sleight of hand.

He goes on to say that *"long ago the Christian Fathers condemned those who practised the more demoralising legerdemain, the art of magic, and astrology"*, hereby seemingly drawing a distinction between legerdemain (a word composed of the French 'léger de main', or sleight of hand) and other segments of the 'art of magic'.

While these mentions and discussions of magic as it relates to the medieval period serve to give us a few clues as to

---

[9] As I started out my career in showbusiness as an actor shortly before I became a magician, I ought to include that John of Salisbury describes actors in the following glowing terms:

"I do not, however, assert that the actor is dishonorable when he follows his profession, although it is undoubtedly dishonorable to be an actor."

the continuation of magical performances on some small scale, it is clear that the attitude to magic of all forms means we will likely never know just how many people were performing magic tricks throughout this period, or what effect it would have.

Sadly, there is a far darker consequence of this condemnation of magic in the form of accusations, trials, and executions for the crime of witchcraft.

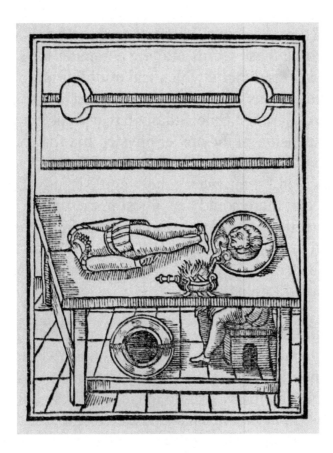

The Discoverie of Witchcraft

In the year 1584, a crucial moment in the history of magic arrived. Not with an incredible new trick that changed the face of magical performance or a hugely famous magician whose name echoes down the ages. I would be surprised if more than a small number of my audience recognised the name of the person who created this crucial moment, and of those who do, the majority will be my fellow magicians.

The name of this man is Reginald Scot.

"Who is Reginald Scot?" I hear you ask, which is worrying as I am typing these words into my computer long before you will ever read them, which leaves only four possibilities for my way of thinking. Either your voice has echoed back through time, although that would require both a suspension of the law of physics and for you to be in the habit of asking questions aloud of the books you are reading, which I think we can both agree is unlikely. Alternatively, there could be a ghost in the room. However, if they were to be reading over my shoulder, they could just as easily have read my notes before I began typing this chapter, in which case they would already know precisely who Reginald Scot is.

The third possibility, of course, is that I am hearing voices in my head, which, although not impossible, would lead me to wonder why the voices in my head have nothing more interesting to say than to make inquiries about a Sixteenth Century man. This leads me to conclude, having eliminated all other possibilities, that hearing you ask the question 'Who is Reginald Scot?' may have been nothing more than a lazy and clichéd rhetorical device, followed by far too much introspection on my part. We may, however, be going off-topic here, so let us return to Reginald Scot himself.

Reginald Scot was born sometime around 1538 in England and died in 1599. If you are anything like me, you may not have a specific idea of what things were like in those years, except that it was back in 'Ye Olde Times', somewhere after the Romans and before the Industrial Revolution. It might help a little more if I were to tell you that he lived in

Tudor England, especially if you went to school in England before 2014[10].

Reginald Scot lived through four monarchs of England, Wales, and Ireland[11], Henry VIII, Edward VI, Mary I, and Elizabeth I[12], and his book was written during the reign of the last of these monarchs, which means that he lived through a time where religion was a tumultuous subject, and caught up in this was the subject of superstition and witchcraft.

For those of you not in the UK, who didn't learn about the Tudors in school, or whose knowledge of Henry the Eighth is restricted to his six wives, and whose knowledge of Elizabeth I comes from Blackadder II[13], it is probably worth a quick overview of the religious turbulence which happened through the reigns of these monarchs.

We really must begin before Scot's birth, with the first of the Tudor monarchs, Henry VII, who became King of England in 1485 after defeating Richard III at the Battle of Bosworth Field. He then went on to have six children, the

---

[10] I checked on the internet while writing this chapter, and discovered that since 2014 'The Tudors' has no longer been part of the National Curriculum. I assume this means there will now be whole generations of children who don't get to experience the joy of putting on an itchy 'Tudor' outfit and going to spend the day walking round an old historic building while reenactors pretend not to understand what a 'camera' or a 'bus' is.

[11] It would be less than four years after Scot's death that James VI of Scotland united the crowns of Scotland, Wales, Ireland and England.

[12] Not counting Lady Jane Grey, who was hailed by some as Queen for nine days between Edward VI and Mary I and was executed in 1554 at the age of just 17. Sadly, this will not be the last execution in this chapter.

[13] Which, thanks to the wonderful Mrs Turner, was the jumping off point for a fair amount of the history that I learned in secondary school.

oldest of which, Arthur, was the heir to his throne and was married to Catherine of Aragon in 1501 at the age of fifteen, but then sadly died the following year in 1502.

This meant that Henry VII's second son, Henry, suddenly found himself heir to the throne, and, as the marriage between Catherine and Arthur had been politically arranged, also heir to his deceased brother's wife.

The young Henry became King Henry the Eighth in 1509 and was on the throne through Scot's childhood years until the King died in 1547.

The King is famous for his six wives, who in order were divorced, beheaded, and then the third died as a result of childbirth, then the rest were divorced, beheaded and survived. Therefore King Henry is most infamous for his six wives, and one reason which is often given for the fact that he kept changing wives is that he was desperate for a strong male heir to continue his line of succession when he was gone. This did not work out as he had hoped, as following his death, his son Edward ruled for just over six years, followed (controversially) by Lady Jane Grey for nine days, who was then executed for high treason. Then Mary I took the throne for a period of just over five years, and then Elizabeth I became the final Tudor monarch in 1558.

Three (or four if you count Jane Grey) monarchs in just over ten years is not a solid line of succession. Added to this that King Henry VIII had broken away from the Catholic Church in Rome by declaring himself the head of

The Church in England (officially marked by the 1834 Act of Supremacy), following which the Pope excommunicated the king.

This created a split between the Catholics and Protestants in England and Wales, which led to the deaths of many people over the course of the Tudor dynasty. However, whether they were Protestant or Catholic, all were in agreement that 'devil worship' or witchcraft was against God.

Henry's biggest act in specific relation to the history of magic was in 1541 when the first Witchcraft Act was passed, which the UK Parliament's website records as *'an act against Conjurations, Witchcrafts, Sorcery and Inchantments'*. This defined Witchcraft as a crime punishable in the worst instances by death, although the act was repealed by Edward in 1547.

It was under the reign of Elizabeth I that witchcraft was once again outlawed, and the use of witchcraft was made punishable by imprisonment, or execution in cases where the witch's actions had led to a death. These executions were not carried out through burning, as popular culture can sometimes make us think, but rather through hanging.

Witches were put on trial in England up until 1717, when the last trials took place in Leicester. The worst period of witch trials took place from 1560-1700 in the South East of England, during which time 513 witches were put on trial with a total of 112 executed, and an estimated total of 500 people (mostly women) executed across England for witchcraft, which leaps up to estimates of more than 30,000 between 1427 and 1782 globally.

It was in the era of the worst witch trials in South-East England, in 1584, when Reginal Scot released a book called 'A Discoverie of Witchcraft'.

Given what I have written above about the witch trials, you would be forgiven for assuming that this was a book designed to teach an upcoming witchfinder the best ways to root out and discover signs of a witch, but it is actually the opposite. The book rather seeks to show that a rational consideration of the subject would prove that witchcraft was not real and gives details of many of the superstitions about witchcraft that he believed to be erroneous and which he hoped would help to move people away from the ideas that led to the witch trials.

One section of the book, however, gives us our interest in Scot, from 'The Twelfe Chapter[14], which has the title *'Of illusions, confederacies and legierdemaine and how they may be well or ill-used.'*

In this chapter, we have an important argument made for the fact that these magic tricks are not something that can be considered in the realms of witchcraft, and show that magic was being performed at that time, as it is on many occasions today, with the aim of bringing joy to people.

---

[14] Yes, that is how 'twelth' is spelt in my copy of the work.

"Howbeit, if these things be doone for mirth and recreation, and not to the hurt of our neighbour, nor to the abusing or prophaning of Gods name, in mine opinion they are neither impious nor altogether unlawfull: though herein or hereby a naturall thing be made to seeme supernaturall. Such are the miracles wrought by jugglers, consisting in fine and nimble conveiance, called legierdemaine: as when they seeme to cast awaie, or to deliver to another that which they reteine still in their owne hands."

What sets Scot's work aside from the descriptions of tricks which we have seen earlier in the book, is that the chapter goes on not only to describe tricks, but actually to give away the method as well, in such a way that the reader could go away and recreate the tricks if they wanted to. It is those descriptions of the method that makes this a new kind of book, the first 'magic book' from which students of the art can learn the tricks.

I am a big fan of magic books. I own quite a number, and I am always on the lookout for more, and I try to read through every single one (although I must admit to being somewhat behind in my reading of those books from the time I have spent diving into books containing magical history), and whenever I meet anyone who expresses an interest in learning magic, my advice to them is to start by buying magic books, rather than learning from DVDs or videos on YouTube.

This isn't because I am a luddite who is afraid of new technology (I certainly am not), nor is it because I am a little old-fashioned (I certainly am). There is a rational reason why I suggest this, and it comes down to my enjoyment of seeing unique performances from different magicians.[15]

When you watch a performer teaching you a trick, the first time you get to know the trick is through that performer, meaning your first visualisation of the moves, the words, and the gestures, are of this person performing them. This is likely to subconsciously affect your performance of the trick itself, and you will have started by surrendering part of your personality to theirs.

Compare that to sitting down with a book to learn a magic trick. Unencumbered by the vision of somebody else performing the trick, you sit and read how the trick will be performed. You turn the words and pictures into actions, first in your head and then with your own hands as you practice the moves. Right from the beginning, the only person you visualise performing this trick is you, and as a result, the performance will be much more your own.

As for which books you should read, I have included some recommendations in 'Further Reading' later in this book.

I will leave the subject of future magicians for now and head back to Reginald Scot and his magic book. I will be honest and say that while I think the book, and certainly

---

[15] I think I first heard this rational explained by the great Paul Daniels in an interview some years ago, but I have heard it expressed by other performers since then, and I am not sure who the thought originally belongs to. That said, I profoundly agree with it.

from Chapter 'Twelfe' onwards, is worth reading if you have an interest in the subject, I wouldn't recommend that someone who has been inspired by this book to learn a magic trick or two[16] rush out to get a copy of 'The Discoverie of Witchcraft', as you will find that the language is archaic and can be hard to read for a modern audience, and takes some time to get into, much like when watching a Shakespeare play it can take a while to attune to the style of writing.

However, that is not to say that there aren't good tricks contained within the pages. For example, in Chapter 23, we get to learn about *'the ball, and the manner of legierdemaine therewith'*. This includes a trick which requires three or four balls *'and as manie small candlesticks, bolles, saltsellers or saltseller covers, which is the best.* That's right, this is another variation of our old friend, the cups and balls, carried all the way from Ancient Greece and Rome to Sixteenth Century England.

If cups and balls are a staple of magic in the modern era, perhaps just as much so are effects involving money. One of the latest additions to my magical inventory is a wonderful trick created by the 20th Century magic creator Jack Hughes, whose effect is to make coins pass through an upturned pint glass and land in a shot glass inside, in view of the audience.

---

[16] If you have been, please let me know, whether in a review or with an email, it would be lovely to hear.

The tricks in Scot's book may be more rudimentary than this and yet could prove just as effective if the proper performance is created by them.

At this point, I am going to share with you one of the shorter money effects from the book, which I hope you will consider trying out for yourself, and I will update it a little with my notes as well. For this part, I shall put Scot's writings in bold, with my additions in italics.

WITH WORDS TO MAKE A TESTOON TO LEAPE OUT OF A POT, OR TO RUN ALONGST *UPON A TABLE.*

You shall see a juggler take a groat or a testoon – *these are both coins from the days when the book was written. To use these coins today would be to immediately spark suspicion, when one of the reasons coin magic is so popular is its use of everyday objects. I would recommend replacing these coins with a shiny fifty-pence or ten-pence pieces as they are large enough to see clearly but do not have the weight of a £2 coin.*[17] – **and throwe it into a pot, or laie it in the midst of a table, & with inchanting words cause the same to leape out of the pot, or run towards him, or from him ward alongst the table.** - *At this point, I hope you understand the effect, but I will clarify in modern language. The coin is taken and either thrown into a pot or cup, or just laid on the table, at which point it climbs out of the pot or cup, or moves across the table, or even moves away from the table.* - **Which will**

---

[17] Obviously if you are outside of the UK then these coins may be suspicious where you live, so use some local currency.

seeme miraculous, untill you knowe that it is doone with a long blacke haire of a woman's head, fastened to the brim of a groat, by meanes of a little hole driven through the same with a Spanish needle. – *The method behind this trick is, as the saying goes, simple, but not easy. As you can see, Scot recommends that this trick be achieved by drilling a small hole through the coin and then tying a long black hair through the hole to enable the coin to be pulled across the table. My hair is long, but nowhere near as long as Felicity's. However, I don't feel she would take kindly to me plucking out a hair every time I wanted to do this trick. So using a very fine thread[18] will achieve the same result, especially if the tabletop matches the colour of the thread. Scot also suggests making a hole in the coin, but I would recommend attaching the thread with a small piece of blu-tack or a small ball of double-sided tape. This would allow you to remove the thread from the coin secretly at the conclusion of the trick and immediately hand the coin out for examination.* - **In like sort you may use a knife, or anie other small thing: but if you would have it go from you, you must have a confederate, by which meanes all juggling is graced and amended.** – *As Scot points out, you could use any other object. The lighter the object you use, of course, the thinner thread you can use and the less likely it is to break, although a heavier object will seem more magical when it moves, which is a compromise you must decide on. In my opinion the coin is the perfect object for this trick to be performed with, as it is so familiar to everybody. You could also have a 'confederate' or, as magicians would term it in more*

---

[18] If you really want to make the trick its best then consider visiting a magic store and enquiring about invisible thread.

modern times, an assistant who can make the coin move away from you, but in my opinion that is making the effect too complicated and does not really add anything extra from the point of view of the audience.

Now you have a magic trick that you can go away and practice, taken straight out of the first magic book, written more than four centuries ago.

I must admit that I took a break from writing this chapter at this point to go away and have a little play with this trick myself, and I have a few subtleties to add which will help you to sell the overall effect.

First of all, if you prepare the thread with a small rolled-up piece of double-sided tape on one end, you can conceal this in your hand and then perform the effect with a borrowed coin. Simply ask someone if you can borrow a 50-pence piece, and as you take it, give it a squeeze in your hand to affix the tape. As you will remove the tape at the end of the effect, this means that the coin is 'clean' at the start and end of the trick and seemingly removes the possibility of there being something attached to the coin.

The second suggestion I would make is one dealing with misdirection. When you first attempt this, you will immediately notice that if you move the hand holding the end of the thread and the coin follows it, then it will be easy for your audience to conclude that you are somehow pulling the coin with that hand, whether they see the thread or not. So how can we misdirect people away from the movement of that hand?

Imagine you have the loose end of the thread in your right hand and the end containing the double-sided tape in your left. You ask a member of your audience to lend you a coin which you take in your left hand and attach the thread to it with the tape before placing it on the table. As you place the coin on the table, however, you pick up a loop of thread over your left forefinger.

At this point, you have a piece of thread which runs from the coin and loops around the base of your left forefinger and to your right hand. If the coin sits on the table between your two fingers, therefore, then moving your right hand away from the coin will cause the coin not to move towards that hand, but instead towards your stationary left hand.

This is where the presentation must come in. Tell a story to explain why the coin might move. Is it an experiment into the power of the mind or a demonstration of 'The Force' from Star Wars?

Whatever story you tell, it is time for the acting. Put your focus on the coin and your left hand, tensing the hand as though it is transmitting a great force to attract the coin towards it. The combination of your attention showing the audience where to look, and the apparent effort in your left hand, will leave your relaxed right hand completely outside of the audience's sphere of attention, and as long as you are subtle in its movements, no one will be looking towards that hand for an explanation at all.

I hope you will try out this little effect, even if just for yourself, to enjoy performing for yourself a version of a trick from the world's oldest magic book.

The book doesn't stop with tricks involving balls or coins but goes on to explain card tricks, tricks with handkerchiefs, but also what we might think of now as 'stage illusions' such as the one shown in the image at the start of this chapter, supposedly being a demonstration of John the Baptist with his head removed.

If you have ever seen the 'magic colouring book', a favourite of many children's magicians, where a book appears first empty, then filled with line drawings, and then filled with full-colour versions, then you have seen another trick which can be traced all the way back to Reginald Scot's 'The Discoverie of Witchcraft', in which he explains *'How to make a booke, wherein you shall shew everie leafe therein to be white, blacke, blew, red, yellow, greene, &c.'*

It is just a shame that this book did not have the effect that Scot had clearly hoped for in stopping the superstitions which led to the witch trials, as in 1604, five years after Scot's death and twenty years after his book, the first of the Stewart Monarchs, James I of England and Wales and VI of Scotland brought in a new Witchcraft Act strengthening the anti-witchcraft laws and making it a capital offence to commune with or summon evil spirits, regardless of whether harm is caused by the accused 'witch'.

Cosmic Xposure

A Perfectly Ordinary Deck of Cards

One item which has become synonymous with magicians, certainly over the past couple of hundred years, is the 'perfectly ordinary deck of cards[19]'. As we read at the end of the previous chapter, Reginald Scot even included several card tricks in 'The Discoverie Of Witchcraft' – which we shall return to a little later in the chapter.

---

[19] By the way, if you ever do a card trick, try not to tell people it is a perfectly ordinary deck of cards. All you are doing by that is putting the idea in their heads that there may be decks of cards which aren't perfectly ordinary. Show them they are ordinary cards, let them see they are all different by all means, but saying it has the same effect as walking into a room and telling someone you didn't eat their Mars Bar. Why would you make that statement out of nowhere unless you were trying to cover up that you ate their Mars? Ok. What I'm saying to that one person who knows who they are, I'm sorry, I may have eaten your Mars.

It only occurred to me as I sat down to write this book that I had no idea when in history playing cards appeared or why they had developed.

Pause for a moment and see if you can imagine when playing cards first appeared or at which point in history they didn't exist. Can you imagine a group of Romans sitting around in their villa playing 'Snap' on their mosaic floors? Did Richard III lose a horse to one of his knights on a game of poker the evening before the Battle of Bosworth Field?

I already knew that they share certain similarities with tarot cards[20], including that both have four 'suits'. I also learned a few interesting facts about a regular deck of playing cards which may surprise you.

First of all, there are a number of numerical connections between the deck of cards and the calendar, some of which are definitive, and others are a slight stretch. There are four suits in a deck of cards, as there are four seasons in a year, and the deck itself contains fifty-two cards (not counting the jokers), and there are 52 weeks in a year.

There are some who go on to claim that the twelve court cards (a king, queen, and jack/knave of each suit) are, therefore, representative of the twelve months of a year. Finally, the total value of all the cards comes to 366, the number of days in a leap year (although you have to count

---

[20] The first records we have are from Northern Italy in the 1440s, at which point in time they were used not as a form of fortune telling as they are often associated with today, but rather as a form of playing cards themselves.

each of the two jokers as one point each to make this work, but with the two jokers there are fifty-four cards instead of fifty-two, so it gets a little shaky at this point).

One historical link between playing cards and magic is in the mystery of their origins. In the same way we don't know who originated the cups and ball trick, we will almost certainly never know who the first person was to perform a magic trick using cards, or even who invented playing cards, or where playing cards were first invented.

Playing cards started to come over to Europe around the turn of the century from the late-1300s to the early-1400s, before which there are suggestions of cards in China, India and other countries, with some suggestions that games involving cards were played in China during the Tang Dynasty (618AD – 904AD), meaning that playing cards in other parts of the world could have pre-dated their arrival in Europe by more than five hundred years.

The first solid description we have of playing cards in Europe comes from a German monk named Johannes von Rheinfelden, who in 1377 wrote a treatise called 'De moribus et disciplina humanae conversationis id est ludus cartularum' ('The game of cards is about the morals and discipline of human behaviour'), in which he explains and describes both the cards and some games, as well as some discussion about the morality within game playing. The fact that he describes and explains the cards holds the suggestion that they were new enough not to be instantly recognisable to everyone and yet were becoming popular enough that he felt the need to write a treatise on the subject.

It is fair to assume that once card games became popular (and particularly when they were played for money) unscrupulous people began to figure out ways to cheat and that the methods they created would have been able to be used by magicians as well to create their tricks. While I never cheat at cards, I have been known to sit around when playing cards and when it is my turn to deal, I shuffle while continuing to have the same card appear at the top of the deck until somebody takes the cards off me, and won't let me shuffle or deal anymore.

It is a Franciscan monk and mathematician who, between 1496 and 1508, gave us our first recorded mention of card tricks in his 'De viribus quantitatis' ('On the Powers of Numbers').

Perhaps it is now time to learn a card trick of your own, and as I don't want to give away someone else's secret, we shall go back to Reginald Scot's 'The Discoverie of Witchcraft' and learn a trick that he revealed back in 1584, where Chapter Seventeen teaches:

"Of cards, with good cautions how to avoid cousenage therein: speciall rules to conveie and handle the cards, and the manner and order how to accomplish all difficult and strange things wrought with cards."

We are going to look at one technique, one method, which will allow you to perform a number of different effects. I shall share one with you, and then I shall allow you to indulge your magical creativity. Let us begin with the basic method from Scot's book.

"In shewing feats, and juggling with cards, the principall point consisteth in shuffling them nimblie, and alwaies keeping one certeine card either in the bottome, or in some knowne place of the stocke, foure or five cards from it. Hereby you shall seeme to worke woonders; for it will be easie for you to see or spie one card, which though you be perceived to doo, it will not be suspected, if you shuffle them well afterwards. And this note I must give you, that in reserving the bottome card, you must alwaies (whilest you shuffle) keepe him a little before or a little behind all the cards'.

The simplest description of this method, therefore, is the goal of shuffling the cards in such a way that they appear to be thoroughly shuffled, and yet the bottom card of the deck, known to you, does not actually change at all. I absolutely agree with Scot's words here that mastery of this simple trick will make it so that *"you shall seeme to worke woonders"*.

There are many ways to shuffle a deck of cards and many ways to control the position of the cards, so we will stick with one of the simpler methods and one which is likely to work best for your first card tricks (although if you want to learn more, be sure to check out the 'Further Reading' section at the end of the book).

The shuffle we are going to do is called the 'Riffle Shuffle', and it can be performed in the hands or on a tabletop. It is a shuffle that I have found a lot of people think looks impressive, while at the same time, it is a shuffle which most people perform quite messily. That, for me, is one of the beauties of this as part of your first card tricks because it won't matter if it looks a little messy.

In fact, it will add to the effect if the shuffle looks a little messy because if someone shuffles the cards in a slightly messy fashion, then it is going to seem a lot less likely that, in the course of that shuffle, they have managed to keep control of the position of any specific card.

In order to begin, you will need a deck of cards. At this stage, any deck of cards will do, although you will find all card tricks easier with a good deck of cards.

My personal preference is a deck of Bicycle Playing Cards from the United States Playing Card Company,[21] although

---

[21] From whom I am not receiving anything for mentioning this fact, although I am always open to having fresh decks of cards sent my way.

I know other magicians who prefer Bee Playing Cards or Tally Ho Circle Backs. I have some decks from each of these manufacturers and I always end up using the bicycle decks when I reach for a deck of cards. They are readily available, and a standard deck won't set you back too much (although they make a huge range of decks in different styles and designs, as the selection of different designs I have lying around testifies!).

A word of warning on working with a brand-new deck of Bicycle Cards. They have what is called an 'air-cushioned finish', which allows them to slide over each other and makes it very easy to do a beautiful spread of cards when you first get them, so you can see the faces of each card evenly separated (and I do get a little over-excited whenever I get the 'new deck feel' when they are fresh).

The downside of this is that the cards will be full of life and ready to escape at a moment's notice, scattering themselves across the floor around you, and encouraging you to learn another technique known as the '52 Card Pickup'.

I will assume you have found a deck of cards at this point in time or can use your imagination and come back to this section of the book when you are ready to take a step into the wonderful world of card magic.

Before we begin, take a moment to look at the face of the bottom card in the deck and commit it to memory. If memory is not your strong suit, and you are going to be practising a lot, I suggest always putting the same card on the bottom while practising.

Place the deck on the table in front of you, face down, and then pick up approximately half the cards in your right hand[22] and place them on the table to the right of the first pile.

Next, take each pile in one hand, with your palm across the top of the deck, your fingers running along the outside edge, and your thumbs touching the inside edge of the deck just below the top corner.

Bring the two halves of the deck towards each other so that the corners where your thumbs lay are almost touching and the decks sit at approximately a ninety-degree angle apart from each other, and place your index finger on top of the cards.

---

[22] If you are left-handed you may find it easier to reverse these instructions, although you will find that for the most part both hands do exactly the same.

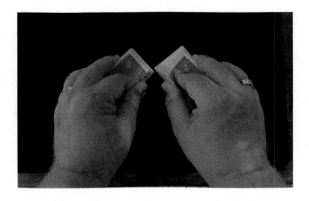

Using your thumbs, gently lift the corners of each half of the deck, and allow the cards to cascade or 'riffle' from your thumbs, weaving together as you do so. As you are doing a magic trick here, the simple secret is to allow the bottom card of the left-hand packet, which was originally the bottom card of the whole deck and, therefore, the card which you have memorised, to slip from your thumb first, before any cards from your right hand.

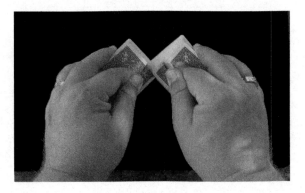

Once all of the cards have cascaded from your thumb, with their corners all now weaved together, place your hands on the bottom edge of the deck and push the two halves together.

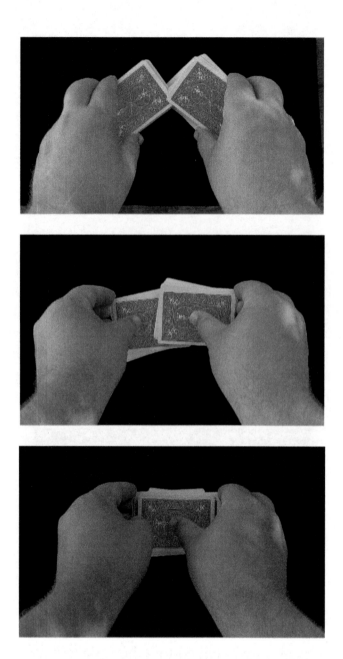

In performing the shuffle like this, you now appear to have mixed up all the cards in the deck while you have secretly retained the bottom card.

Now we know a technique for shuffling the cards while retaining one particular card at the bottom, and we can return to 'The Discoverie of Witchcraft' in order to use this technique within the method of a trick.

"How to tell one what card he seeth in the bottome, when the same card is shuffled into the stocke.

When you have seene a card privilie, or as though you marked it not, laie the same undermost, and shuffle the cards as before you are taught, till your card lie againe below in the bottome. Then shew the same to the beholders, willing them to remember it: then shuffle the cards, or let anie other shuffle them; for you know the card alreadie, and therefore may at anie time tell them what card they saw: which neverthelesse would be done with great circumstance and shew of difficultie."

The method for this particular trick is a great one to start with, as it is relatively simple, which will allow you to work on the overall effect, which is where this trick will sink or swim, and Scot offers up some strong advice on this point.

Let us imagine that you are sitting down with friends or family, about to play a game of cards. Now is the perfect time for some impromptu card magic!

First, ask a member of your small audience to remove any jokers or instruction cards from the deck, and then give them a good shuffle. In terms of the working of the trick, this shuffle is entirely meaningless as we have not yet memorised any cards, but when people recall the trick later, we want them to remember that the cards were shuffled by people other than you, which will help to obscure the method.

Now take the deck of cards and spread them quickly across the table, explaining that you want everyone to check that they are well shuffled, and almost immediately gather the deck back together and place it on the table in front of you.

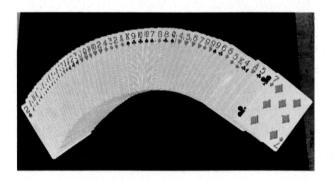

This simple action covers three important moments in the performance of the trick. Firstly, going back to what we said at the start of this chapter, it allows the audience to see that it is a 'perfectly ordinary deck of cards' without you drawing attention to it. It also adds another reminder to the audience of the fact that the cards are 'well shuffled', which we want them to remember at the end. Finally, of course, it gives you a chance to look at and remember the bottom card.

Timing is important here. You want to spread the cards out just long enough that people can see at a glance that they are shuffled but not long enough to give anyone else a chance to notice which card is on the bottom. It is important, as Scot notes, that you should only glance at the bottom card for a moment *as though you marked it not'*.

At this point, you are going to go into the shuffle we learned above, keeping the card at the bottom. You should learn to do this without having to look at your hands, and as you go through the process two or three times, you can look around the audience and say something along the lines of:

"Some studies say that from new deck order, you have to shuffle a deck of cards seven times to get a truly random order, but there are more than eight unvigintillion possible orders to a deck of cards – it is actually an eight followed by sixty-seven zeros."

What you actually say here is up to you, as it has to fit your personality. I like this line, in particular, because it allows you once again to subtly reinforce the random order of the cards, and it is quite fun to say the word 'unvigintillion' – and yes, I did have to look it up. The main purpose of talking here is to draw people's attention away from your shuffle slightly. When they look back on the trick later, we want them to remember that the deck was repeatedly shuffled but not to focus on you shuffling them at this point in the trick.

Now turn to one of the audience members (I would tend to choose someone different from the person who first shuffles the cards to involve more people in the effect), and say to them:

"I am going to look away. When I do, please pick up the whole deck and look at the bottom card. Show it to everyone else, and all remember the card – but please make absolutely certain I can't see the card and that there are no reflections I can see it in. Then shuffle the deck again and make sure your card is completely lost again, so I can't know where it is."

Once again, this sentence can, and should, be adapted to suit your own style, but there are a few key points here again. Make sure the instructions are clear – you don't want people to think they are to pick a random card or anything like that.

The reason we ask them to 'show everybody' is so that the person who sees the card can't lie about it later (which happens very occasionally) and so that if they forget the card (which happens slightly more often), then the rest of the audience will be able to remind them. Telling people to please make sure you can't see it also sends the message that you don't know what the card is already – even though you do!

Turn your back, and allow them to follow these instructions. If you listen carefully, you should be able to hear when they start shuffling the cards, and that is a good time to ask if they are ready.

At this point, the trick is complete – you know which card they chose. Now is the time when 'effect' really gets the chance to shine. If, at that point in time, you just told them their card, then it really would remain just a trick, and it probably wouldn't take them too long to guess something close to the correct solution. The single most important part of any effect is the final impact it leaves the audience with, and the great thing is that at this point in proceedings, you have nothing to worry about.

I will give you one ending to the trick, but I really encourage you to try your own – and if you ever see me at a show, please come and show me your version[23]!

Once the card has been looked at and the deck shuffled, take it back and once again spread the cards face up across the table. Resist the temptation to immediately scan the deck for their card – remember that you are not supposed to know where the card is yet.

Point your index finger downwards, and hold it a few inches above the cards, and explain to your audience that this will be an experiment in the power of group thinking, whether if enough people have the same thought in their head that another person can be influenced by this idea. Ask them all to concentrate on their card, to focus on

---

[23] There are some magicians who worry about performing magic for fellow magicians. Sometimes this is out of fear that the magician will know how it is done and tell people to ruin it. That is not something any magician I have ever met would do – why would we take away that moment of wonder from an audience rather than sharing in the enjoyment?

The other reason, I think, is that they worry that the magician won't enjoy it if they know how it is done. For that I would remind you it is all in the presentation. I have a friend and fellow performer named Mr Alexander who performs, in my opinion, the greatest version of 'The Linking Rings' I have ever seen. Do I know how it is done? Yes. Does that stop me sitting down and watching it every chance I get? No!

guiding your finger towards it, but not to look at the card directly.

Begin to move your finger back and forth along the row of cards, allowing yourself at any point to glance down and locate your target.

Now take your time, enjoy the moment. Slowly lessen the range that your finger travels across the cards as you slowly lower it down. If you time it right, you can have your finger land perfectly on the card as it passes.

Then just push that card forward, and enjoy the reaction.

What do you do if anyone asks how you did it?

You reply, "Very well, thank you."

I hope you enjoy performing your first card trick!

FAWKES,
(Sleight of Hand-man)

Isaac Fawkes and The Egg Bag

As the history of magic moves ever closer to the modern day, we are reaching the point where we have the names and details of some magicians and know some of the tricks they performed, including tricks which have become classics of magic and are still performed by magicians in the modern world, including by myself.

The conjurer I want to talk about from the Eighteenth Century is Isaac Fawkes.

Less than a hundred years following the publication of Reginald Scot's book, Isaac Fawkes was born, in about 1675, although we don't have an exact date of birth for him. In fact, not only do we lack a confirmed date of birth, we actually know little about him until we have the first record of him in the form of advertisements in 1722, about him performing alongside his son who was a tumbler at the Southwark Fair.

Fawkes was a regular performer at both the Southwark Fair and Bartholomew Fairs in London, sometimes performing six shows a day, which were two of the bigger annual fairs on the show circuit. The fact that advertisements were being taken out, and sometimes taken out by Fawkes himself, to advertise his performances at fairs, shows that the art of conjuring had begun to gain some respectability, and these adverts also reveal some details about his act, and even his performances for royalty.

In the advertisement above, for performances at the Blue Boar (clearly not a particularly well-known establishment as he notes that it is *"next door to the Castle Tavern in Fleet Street"*, he is keen to point out that he has performed for "King George, the Prince, and all the Quality of the whole Kingdom with great Applause".

Fawkes was big on self-promotion in this way, which is as much a part of show business today as it was back then although one of his adverts may seem a little strange, and even off-putting, to a modern reader. One advert in 1723 began:

"The famous Mr Fawks, as he modestly styles himself, has since Bartholomew and Southwark-Fairs, put seven hundred Pounds into the Bank."

Ignoring for the moment that the suggestion that there is any modesty when he calls himself 'the famous Mr Fawks',[24] it seems remarkably odd to take out an advert to tell people how much money a performer has just put in their bank. A quick online conversion tool suggests that this amount of money would have a relative value of nearly two hundred thousand pounds today.

Just imagine, for a moment, if Derren Brown's advert for his next show began by telling you his bank balance rather than talking about the show itself. I can't imagine it would be the best way to encourage the audience to come through the doors.

---

[24] As with many figures from the past, we have numerous spellings of his surname, including Fawkes, Fawks and Faux.

On the flip side, however, instead of comparing Fawkes' marketing as a conjurer to that of a conjurer today, what if we instead compare it to the movie business. When a new movie comes out one of the things which is reported on to discuss the success or otherwise of a film is the box office take. One way in which 'Avatar' is looked at in the film industry is that it has currently got the highest box office figures of all time, $2,923,706,026, and is therefore considered by this metric to be the most successful movie of all time, followed by 'Avengers: Endgame' ($2,797,501,328), 'Avatar: The Way of Water' ($2,320,250,281), and Titanic ($2,257,844,554).

The fact that three of these four movies were directed by James Cameron gives us a very similar piece of information to that provided by the announcement that Isaac Fawkes had banked seven hundred pounds, in that it tells us that both performers shared the ability to bring in the crowds.

One of the great things about the advertisements which Fawkes put out, and the most interesting to me, is that they list some of the effects which he will be performing.

"The famous Mr Fawks performs his most surprising Tricks by Dexterity of Hand with his Cards, Eggs, curious Indian Birds, Mice and Money."

Here we have the groundwork for so many classics of modern magic. Although I don't perform with animals, for personal moral reasons, most days that I perform, I will work with cards and money, and often with eggs as well.

Although I have never heard of an act working with 'curious Indian Birds' before, as recently as 2014 one of the runners up on 'Britain's Got Talent' was Darcy Oake who performed a dove act in one of the rounds.

As for mice, there is a lovely story I once heard told by Paul Daniels (who I will be talking about a lot more later on), involving a visit to Las Vegas where he met Lance Burton. Watching a video tape of one of Paul's shows where, in a close up shot, he made a white mouse appear inside a previously empty matchbox, Lance Burton turned to him in a moment of realisation and said, "On television, you don't need a tiger!"

It is one of these props in particular which encouraged me to include Fawkes in this book, and that prop is the egg, and the trick which is done with it, described in a little more detail in a different advert:

"He takes an empty bag, lays it on the Table and turns it several times inside out, then commands 100 Eggs out of it."

The Egg Bag trick is one which you may be familiar with, most famously performed on television in the UK by the great comedy magician Tommy Cooper. If you have never seen Tommy Cooper, it is well worth looking up this effect of his on YouTube, and then (if you are anything like me) falling into a Tommy Cooper 'Youtube Rabbithole'. It was performed previously to that by Max Malini, who really created the classic modern version, but one of its earliest performers was Issac Fawkes in the early 1700s.[25]

This trick is special to me, as the first time I saw it was a few days after I arrived in Italy for my first tour over there in 2007. I did not know then that magic was waiting in the wings to grab hold of me and steer my career down a new path, when I had the chance to watch my new director at the time (now a very dear friend), Rupert, performing a one-man comedy magic show he had written and toured for many years called 'Me and My Chicken'.

I will always remember watching as, part way through the show, he took out a small cloth bag and an egg, placed the egg into the bag, and then moments later turned the bag inside out and spread his hands to show that both the bag and his hands were empty. A moment later he reached into the bag again and pulled the egg back out.

I was 21 years old, and I was genuinely amazed. For that tiny moment in time the world did not fit together! For that moment I wasn't looking for a 'secret', I was just a child again, seeing a moment of magic. The routine and the show continued, but I was held on that moment, and from then on I wanted to learn not just that trick, but as many ways as I could to share that moment with other people.

---

[25] I will not be teaching this effect, despite its age, as it is a working trick in many performer's shows today, and I don't want to take the wonder of the trick away from anyone who doesn't want to know it. If you want to learn it, and some other classic tricks, I can recommend 'Classic Secrets of Magic by Bruce Elliott' which you should be able to find second hand somewhere.

In the end I did learn the Egg Bag trick. Rupert taught it to me, as he taught me much of my early magic, and taught me the whole show, which I took on different tours in Italy for nearly a decade, getting to see that moment of wonder on other people's faces as well. I found different versions of the trick, and I expanded on the trick, and I grew a magical career, and I have been given the opportunity to share magical moments with so many people.

It all began with an egg, a bag, and a trick from three hundred years earlier.

Fawkes himself continued to perform until1732, when, following a fire at one of the fairs he was working at the time, he passed away in May (although it is unclear if the fire was related to his death). It is believed that he may have left his widow as much as ten thousand pounds (just shy of two million pounds today). He had decidedly turned conjuring into a popular entertainment which could turn a performer, if they were skilled and lucky, into a wealthy man.

The Magic Shop

One of my great joys within my work as a magician is the moment when I am preparing a new show, whether for a live performance or one of our videos, and whether for a close-up performance or a large stage, when I get to start looking for new tricks and effects to include, and this means, alongside a look through my magical library, that sooner or later in the process it is time to visit a magic shop. Very often, this means a visit to the shop's website, but whenever possible I make sure to visit the 'bricks and mortar' shops – two of my favourites being 'Merchant of Magic' (pictured above) in Bishops Waltham (UK) and 'Alakazam Magic' in Ashford (UK).[26]

A good magic shop has a special feel to it. You will see tricks all around you, usually with some magical

---

[26]I want to make it clear at this point in time that neither of these companies has in any way paid or compensated me for this mention in the book. However, whether you are a budding magician, an enthusiastic amateur, someone who would just like to learn a couple of tricks, or a working professional magician (who probably knows both of these companies) than I would recommend both as places to get good magic – and good honest advice about which of their effects would suit you.

memorabilia worked in. Most importantly, however, you will have a magician/shopkeeper behind the counter who will be both deeply knowledgeable about magic in general and eager to show you a trick or two. I must admit that I don't think I have ever gone into a magic shop, no matter how carefully I have prepared a list of tricks that I intend to purchase, without having ended up buying at least one more trick that I have been shown by the magician working there.

As we've learned, however, magic was not always seen as a legitimate pastime and that we were well into the 16th Century before even the first magic book came into existence, so we know at that time there were no magic stores to head to. These days there are quite a number of magic stores around the world, both physically and online.

"So how", as Baldrick so succinctly phrased it in Blackadder Goes Forth, *"did we get from the one case of affairs to the other case of affairs?"*

The answer is Mayette Magie Modern in Paris, France.

When Charles Aubert started his business in 1808, he can't have known that it would go on to become the world's first magic shop, and one that is still running today. Part of the reason that he couldn't have known that this is where the business would end up is that the business started not as a magic shop, but as a music publisher.

It wasn't until 1830, when they moved to new premises, that the shop began to sell a few novelties and pieces of equipment designed for conjuring, and then in 1913 a new owner, Henri Billy (who named the shop Billy Maison) started to sell illusions as well.

In the 1930s a magician named André Mayette took over the running of the shop, and now magic became the full focus of the store, now with the name Mayette Magie Modern. Mayette began to publish magic books, and even started a magazine for magicians entitled 'Le Magicien'. The store continues to run to this day, now owned by father and daughter Dominique and Alexandra Duvivier, both magicians. I have never had a chance to visit yet, as I have not yet been to Paris (outside of a trip to EuroDisney), but I shall certainly make a pilgrimage there when I am in the area.

Meanwhile, over in the UK, in 1898, George William John Ryan, who went by the stage name of Lewis Davenport (apparently taken from Davenpord Road in Lewisham), started his own mail order magic company named Davenports and Co.

Setting up the business from scratch at that point in time, 70 years before the first electronic printers, meant that in the early days he wrote out the instructions by hand before sending them out. It wasn't until 1905, when he had the innovative idea of putting an advert into a newspaper, offering to exchange magic tricks for a printing press, that he could mass produce the instructions.

The shop itself remained a family business over the next decade, moving first to New Oxford Street, then to Great

Russel Street opposite the British Museum. Then they moved from the busy tourist routes into a new location, in the underground tunnels between Charing Cross and Trafalgar Square, and it was there I first visited the store, and it really was everything that I wanted a magic shop to be.

Here in the underground tunnels, with the hustle and bustle of London far above, you would find yourself in a flow of tourists, commuters and shoppers as they rushed between tube stations. When you ducked down a side tunnel, however, almost like moving into Diagon Alley from Harry Potter, you were suddenly alone, the crowds of the 'real world' left behind.

Down this tunnel was Davenport's Magic, and the window was filled with a host of magical apparatus and props, including an Egyptian Mummy who I would go on to tour with for a couple of years. When you went through the front door, the shop still felt like it had been fitted out by Lewis Davenport a hundred years ago.

There were shelves filled with magic books, display cases containing tricks new and old, and on the counter lay a close-up mat for the staff to use to demonstrate tricks. There was a door behind the counter, behind which who knew what magic would be happening.

Sadly, in January 2020, Davenports Magic put the following notice up on their Twitter account.

"It is with great regret that we need to announce that Davenports Magic Shop in Charing Cross will be closing for the final time on Thursday, 30th of January 2020. This is due to the redevelopment of the Underground Arcade that we have called home for some 36 years..."

With that 48 word message, Davenports Magic went from its home in the tunnels of the London Underground, into the pages of magical history.

As mentioned above, many magic shops have now moved online, and if you want to become a magician you can certainly find many places who will sell you tricks online, and if you live far away from a magic shop it may be your first option to start with.

If, however, you can find one nearby with a real 'bricks and mortar' shop, I really recommend a visit to what will feel like an Aladdin's Cave of wonder. I particularly recommend those I mentioned at the start of the chapter, as I know from first hand experience how good they are. Talk to the staff behind the counter, let them know what sort of magic you are interested in, and they will be able to point you in the right direction.

Le Carton de Robert-Houdin.

Jean-Eugène Robert-Houdin

Few magicians in this book will get a chapter to themselves, purely on grounds of space.

Still, it is very difficult to overestimate the influence on magic over the past couple of centuries of Jean-Eugène Robert-Houdin, even though there are many people outside of the magic community who may not have ever heard his name (although you are likely to be familiar with a magician who commandeered his name, Houdini).

Before I get onto his story and those of some of the other magicians in the coming chapters dealing with those magicians of the nineteenth and early-twentieth centuries, I want to address one of the more problematic questions to face anyone embarking on writing history, and anyone writing a history which speaks in fond or admiring tones about the people being discussed.

Unfortunately, in the nineteenth and early-twentieth centuries, a lot of attitudes, opinions, laws and social norms were not as they are today[27], and this will be reflected in the actions of some of those people whom I will be writing about.

I will, in a later chapter, be regaling you with some details about the Chinese magician named Chung Ling Soo, who was actually a Scottish magician named William Robinson – certainly displaying a level of 'cultural appropriation', and sometimes in ways which could easily be seen as racist to a modern audience.

My good friend Jem Duducu[28], history writer and host of the podcast 'Condensed Histories' (which I produce for him and can strongly recommend), always talks about the dangers of looking at history in the wrong direction and applying modern sensibilities to people in the past.

As such, I will try not to shy away from some of the more difficult actions of these magicians where they form an integral part of the story, but at the same time, I think that they deserve their place in the history of magic, and in

---

[27] Or, to put it a much more optimistic way, we have come along way in the last couple of hundred years.

[28] Jem named a character after me in one of his historical novels, 'Echoes', so it seems only fair that I mention him in my book in return!

some cases deserve to be honoured for their role in enhancing this aspect of the performing arts.

This will be the case in this chapter about Robert-Houdin, a man who marks a big step forward with the art of the magician, and yet at the same time used his tricks in the service of the French Government to assist in the oppression of the native people in the French colony of Algeria.

With Robert-Houdin, I want to mostly give you an 'origin story', much as you get with most superhero movies, for I think how Robert-Houdin became a magician is as interesting as his time as a magician. In his memoirs, 'Confidences d'un Prestidigiteur'[29], Robert-Houdin begins his life story with the words:

"I commence by stating to my readers, with a certain degree of pride, that I was born at Blois, the birthplace of Louis XII., surnamed the "Father of his People," and of Denis Papin, the illustrious inventor of the steam engine. So much for my native town. As for my family, it would only appear natural, regard being had to the art to which I devoted my life, that I should display in my family tree the name of Robert le Diable, or of some medieval sorcerer; but, being the very slave of truth, I will content myself with stating that my father was a watchmaker."

While Robert-Houdin suggests here that 'a watchmaker' was not a family link which would lend itself to the

---

[29] In the English translation of this book in my collection, this is translated as 'Memoirs of Robert-Houdim, Ambassador, Author and Conjurer'.

ancestry of a magician, yet without this being his father's profession, it seems unlikely to me that Robert-Houdin would have become a magician of as much fame as he would go on to build, and indeed, it was only through a mistake during his time watchmaking that he developed an interest in magic at all.

Jean was born in December 1805, and from early childhood he grew up with an interest in his father's work and would amuse himself with files and hammers, and confesses in his memoirs that:

"I need not say that my excellent mother had frequently to wipe away the young mechanic's tears, when the hammer, badly directed, struck my fingers."

It could easily have been that this interest would have sustained Robert-Houdin through his entire life and that he could have been quite content to live out his life as a watchmaker, a trade which he did practise for many years.

A childhood illness for a time meant that the young Jean Robert (for he did not become Robert-Houdin until he married and added his wife's surname to his own) was forced to rest. He also had a kind neighbour named Mr Bernard, a colonel who had once been a prisoner for a number of years and during that time had learned to make a range of toys, a skill which he taught to Jean Robert. Far more importantly, in my opinion, he also once made a comment which boosted the young boy's confidence and which the magician would go on to remember for all his life.

"I fancy I can still see and hear this old soldier, when, passing his hand over his heavy grey moustache, he exclaimed with energetic satisfaction, "Why, the young scamp can do anything he likes." This compliment flattered my childish vanity, and I redoubled my efforts to deserve it."

This joint interest in crafting 'toys' and watchmaking laid the foundation for two of the main elements of his life's work, but for the third, there was more of a wait.

Jean's father wanted his son to have a good education and the opportunity to earn more than he could following in his father's footsteps as a watchmaker, and so at eleven years of age he was sent to study in a college in Orleans, about forty miles from his birthplace in Blois.

He did not take well to schooling, declaring that the happiest day he ever had there was the day he left. In his free time, however, Jean continued his interest in mechanics and machinery, on one occasion creating a series of mechanisms powered by a number of mice which he caught around the school.

"I had built for them a charming open cage, in which I had fixed up a miniature gymnastic machinery. My prisoners, while taking their ease, set in motion a variety of machines, which caused a most agreeable surprise."

Following his time at college, which he left at eighteen, he gained work in a solicitor's office back home in Blois as a copying clerk. This meant that every day, in a world long before photocopiers, he would have to write out multiple copies of other people's work, much of which he didn't even understand. The tedium of the job on such a creative mind must have taken its toll, and this continued when his next job turned out to be as little more than an errand boy.

An aviary of canaries in the office was to end Jean Robert's time in the office, as he not only fed and cleaned the birds, as was his job, but also began to add baths and pumps, and other mechanical amusements of his own design. In the end, it was noticed that he was spending the majority of his time working with the birds and their cage, and less time on his actual work. Eventually, he was given a warning by his master, Monsieur Roger, that he had to either give up the 'mechanical fancies', or lose his job.

A kindly man, Monsieur Rogers then added:

"And now, my friend, will you let me give you a piece of advice? I have studied you, and feel convinced you will never be more than a very ordinary clerk, and, consequently, a still more ordinary notary, while you might become an excellent mechanician. It would be, then, wiser for you to give up a profession in which you have such slight prospect of success, and follow that for which you evince such remarkable aptitude.

Your father fancied he was acting for the best by putting you in a profession more lucrative than his own; he thought he should only have a simple boyish fancy to overcome, but I am persuaded it is an irresistible vocation, against which you should no longer struggle. I will see

your parents to-morrow, and I have no doubt I shall
induce them to change their opinion about your future
prospects in life."

This seemed to set the course of the young Robert's life, as
he took up an apprenticeship with his cousin to become a
watchmaker and to truly learn the trade in which he had
held such an interest.

I mentioned at the beginning of the chapter that I wanted to
discuss Robert-Houdin's origin story, and it is that task
that has led us to this point. Every superhero has a moment
where they are set on their course. For the young Peter
Parker this is being bitten by a radioactive spider to
become Spiderman. For Bruce Wayne it is the murder of
his parents that sets him on the road to becoming
Batman.[30] For Jean Robert, it was a visit to a bookshop!

The young apprentice watchmaker went, one evening, to a
bookshop to buy a two volume work called 'Treatise on
Watchmaking', when the bookseller, his mind occupied on
other things, hastily handed over the books from a shelf
and took Jean Robert's money.

It was only when he got back to his home that Robert
realised that there had been a mistake, and that one of the
books he had been given held the curious title of
'Scientific Amusements'.

---

[30] At this point I believe I have used up all of my superhero origin story
knowledge, but hopefully you can fill in some more examples if you need them.

Intrigued, he opened the book and was drawn to some of the chapter titles listed within the contents, such as *"The way of performing tricks with the cards"* and *"How to guess a person's thoughts"*.

This was the moment that was to lead Robert down a new path of investigation in life, as he began to read the book, and found that he was hooked. Like sitting down to watch an episode of a series on Netflix, and finding yourself, at three in the morning, suddenly realising you had reached the end of the series, or the day that 'Harry Potter and the Goblet of Fire' was released and I got so engrossed in reading it on a beach in Jersey that my legs got sunburnt to the point where I could barely stand, Jean Robert read on and on.

After some hours of poring over the book, imagining enacting the magic that was contained therein, he was halted by the sudden realisation that the candle whose light he was reading by had burned right down, and the small amount of light that came through the window from the streetlamp outside was not sufficient to read by.

He tried to sleep, so that he could continue the next day, and when sleep wouldn't come he even got the thought in his head to attempt to 'borrow' the street lamp and take it up to his room, planning to lower the lamp, and then to hide it within a hat to hide the light as he snuck home, a plan which went wrong when a baker came out of his shop nearby and started to smoke, leaving Jean Robert hiding in a doorway, cold and scared, until he eventually ran all the way home.

Luckily, this ended his life of crime, but his life of magic had begun, as from that book, and with time and practise, he began his journey towards becoming a magician.

As Robert-Houdin would later write in his memoirs about this occasion:

"The resemblance between two books, and the hurry of a bookseller, were the most common-place causes of the most important event in my life."

He carried on watchmaking for a while longer, with magic as his pastime, and would perform at social events, including one at which he met Josèphe Cecile Houdin, who he fell in love with instantly, and who, on the 8th July 1830, he married, adding her surname to his own to become Jean-Eugène Robert-Houdin.

Robert-Houdin continued to work as a watchmaker, spending his free time working on his magic, or building clockwork automatons which would eventually become a part of his show, or attending the shows of magicians who came on tour to Paris, while all the time dreaming of the day that he might open his own theatre.

Sadly, his first wife passed away in 1843 after a long illness, leaving him with three children, and he remarried not long after, to François Marguerite Olympe Braconnier.

It took until the 3rd July 1845, at forty years of age, before Robert-Houdin achieved his goal of opening his own theatre, the 200-seat 'Théâtre Robert-Houdin' with the first performance of what he called his 'Soirées fantastiques'.

The opening night at the theatre, by Robert-Houdin's own admission, did not go well. It started off fairly, with some friends in the audience offering support. Long nights and overworking to open the theatre, added to this being the accumulation of his dream, allowed his nerves to get the better of him. From his memoirs:

"The thought had suddenly struck me; 'Suppose I were to fail!' And immediately I began to talk quick, hurried on in my anxiety to finish, felt confused, and, like a tired swimmer, I flourished about without being able to emerge from the chaos of my ideas.

Oh! Then I experienced a torture, an agony which I could not describe, but which might easily become mortal were it prolonged.

The real public were cold and silent, my friends were foolish enough to applaud, but the rest remained quiet. I scarcely dared to look around the room, and my experiment ended I know not how.

I proceeded to the next, but my nervous system had reached such a degree of irritation that I no longer knew what I said or did. I only felt that I was speaking with extraordinary volubility, so that the four last tricks of my performance were done in a few minutes.

The curtain fell very opportunely; my strength was exhausted; but a little longer and I should have to crave the indulgence of my audience."

The description, for a performer or anyone who can empathise with one, is uncomfortable reading. I count myself very lucky that I have never suffered stagefright, which I put down to having first been on a stage sleeping in a cot when I was only weeks old, although I do feel the buzz of excitement before a show which, in some ways, is the other side of the same coin.

I have, however, had bad shows, and I think every performer has. Not necessarily when a trick has gone wrong,[31] but there have been occasions, for example, where my peformance has been mis-advertised.

I remember when I performed my first one-man show in the UK, back in 2010, and it was a ninety-minute show themed around the history of Britain, told through magic and comedy.

Imagine my surprise when I turned up at the venue, who had been sent posters from me which they were supposed to use which explained the show, to see that they had created their own posters and decided to sell the event as 'An Evening of Stand-Up Comedy with Greg Chapman', which meant that I walked out on stage to an audience who weren't there to hear anything about history, and weren't

---

[31] Felicity has often claimed that some of her favourite moments in my shows have been times when she has noticed something go wrong, and enjoys seeing my improvising brain cut in to deal with it.

there to see a magic show. They were there to drink and see stand-up comedy.

A short while into the show I realised that this was the case, that the show was going over very badly, and I had to regroup, entirely alter the show, and get through the hour and a half by improvising comedy and re-theming my tricks to work for the audience. I came off stage exhausted, deflated, and vowing never to return to that venue.

Luckily, both Robert-Houdin and I bounced back, and I actually think that, hard reading though it is, that this page from the memoir is a good one for anyone starting out in performing arts to consider, a reminder that even the greatest performers have to start somewhere, and that allowing doubt and nerves to overtake you can be damaging no matter what level you reach.

The theatre struggled along for its first few years, with Robert-Houdin gaining confidence and refining his performance abilities at every step, and getting good responses from the critics, but not quite being able to get enough 'bums on seats', especially during the summer months, to make for a profitable enterprise. He even had to sell three houses that he had inherited to keep the theatre open.

What changed his fortunes was a trick he created and performed with his son, Émile, which he called 'Second Sight'.

'Second Sight', being the ability to view distant objects that you would not normally be able to see, would involve Robert-Houdin entering the audience and being handed items, which his son, sat on the stage, would then name. This type of effect on its own is not new, there is even a version in 'The Discoverie of Witchcraft', but Robert-Houdin's version captured the public's attention as it modified over time to make it seem more and more impossible.

Robert-Houdin would ring a bell rather than speaking, so that he couldn't be sending secret coded messages in what he said, or gave his son a glass of water, and sipping it, Émile would tell people what drink it tasted like, matching a drink that a member of the audience was thinking of.

This one trick started the crowds coming in to the theatre, and with the development of other tricks like the 'Marvellous Orange Tree' or the 'Light-Heavy Chest' made his name, and from then on he performed in his

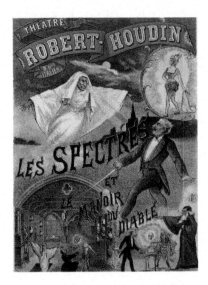

theatre and on tour until his final tour in 1855, following which he retired to write his memoirs and various books on magic until his death in 1871.

Coming back to the beginning of this chapter, however, there was one more tour that Robert-Houdin was to make following his official retirement in 1855, when, in 1856, he was asked by the French Government, by the president, Napoleon III, to go on tour to French occupied Algeria to assist the French Army in pacifying the region to ensure French control of the territory, and this is the time I was referring to at the start of the chapter when I spoke of attitudes in the past being different from those today.

Napoleon III was worried about local tribal leaders called the Marabouts, who used superstition and 'magic' to keep control of their people, and who would pose a serious problem for French rule if they decided to instruct their tribes to rise up against the French Army.

Napoleon decided that the logical answer to that would be to send France's greatest magician over to Algeria to show them the strength of the French Magic.

It is in these shows that one of the worst uses of magic was committed, in that a performance of magic tricks, while claiming they were real, was being used to control a population.

In his performance, Robert-Houdin presented the 'light-heavy chest'. Bringing out the strongest member of a tribe, he would have the tribesman lift the chest, which he would easily.

Then, waving his wand and showing another way in which times were different in terms of what it was acceptable to say, he would declare:

"Behold! Now you are weaker than a woman; try to lift the box."

When the tribesman again tried to lift the box, it would not move, no matter how much strength he put into it. If it looked likely the handles would be pulled off, Robert-Houdin had also rigged the box so that he could deliver an electric shock, forcing the poor challenger to let go.
At another performance for a group of tribal leaders, Robert-Houdin also demonstrated a bullet catch, having a signed bullet fired at him which he then caught in his teeth.[32]

With the power of French Magic ascertained, Robert-Houdin returned to France and to his retirement.

I certainly do not agree with this period of the magician's life, magic should be used to bring joy and entertainment, and not as part of a strategy of oppression. I hope, however, that people can look past this, understand the actions as they fitted into the time, and reflect that in this instance, where otherwise the French Army may have put down potential uprisings in far more brutal manners.

---

[32] It should go without saying, do not try this at home. Even if you know the method this trick is incredibly dangerous, as we will learn in a later chapter.

Robert-Houdin's legacy as a magician lives on, he helped bring the art of magic to big theatres, and popular attention, and he even created the image of the magician which was to run well into the Twentieth Century, with a tailcoat and top hat, an image which influenced my old-fashioned style in my show outfits.

He also inspired the most famous magician of all time, Harry Houdini, although you will have to wait a little longer to learn more about him.

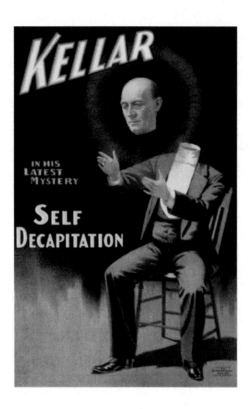

The Great Victorian Magicians

When Queen Victoria took to the throne in 1837, Robert-Houdin hadn't yet opened the Palais Royale, and yet by the time she passed away in 1901, Harry Houdini was on tour around Great Britain and theatre magic really was into its 'Golden Age' leading into the start of the Twentieth Century.

In the 63 years and 216 days of Victoria's reign, a period which I will be referring to as the Victorian Era, regardless of where in the world I am talking about, there are many magicians and magical names to talk about.

I have selected three magicians born during her reign, even though many went on beyond her death, and I offer my apologies to all of the great magicians of the era who I have left out, for there are far too many to include them all.

So without further ado, I shall turn the spotlight onto the first of our Great Victorian Magicians!

Harry Kellar
1849 – 1922

Much like Robert-Houdin in the last chapter, Harry Keller's rise to reach a stage where he is referred to as the 'Dean of American Magicians', and where the online version of the 'Encyclopaedia Britannica' refers to him as the *"first great magician native to the United States"* wasn't one that ran smoothly or was devoid of financial issues.

When he was just ten years old, and working in a drugstore, the young Kellar was experimenting with chemicals when he damaged the floor of the shop and, not wanting to have to face the music when his parents found out, he hopped a train to New York, where he was taken in by a minister, who began to train Kellar up for that line of work.

When he was twelve years old, Kellar saw an advert in a newspaper placed there by I.H Hughes, a magician who performed as the 'Fakir of Ava' who was looking for an assistant. Kellar had previously seen the magician perform, and had dreamed of becoming a magician since then, and so he took the job and went on to spend the next six years gaining an apprenticeship as he toured around with the older magician, learning about magic and show business.

While he may have learned the magic well, it appears he hadn't quite got the hang of the business side of things, because when, in 1867, Kellar set off on his own to take his magic show on tour around the Midwest, he ended up having to hand all of his equipment over to people who he had borrowed money from, and once again he got on a train, this time heading for Wisconsin.

It was here that he sidestepped in his career again, as he met the 'Davenport Brothers and Fay', magicians who performed a stage spiritualism act, and who we will talk about in a later chapter, and became their manager, helping to organise their tours and, in the process, learning the secrets of their act, and about how to correctly structure a show.

In 1873, Kellar quit the show after a falling out with William Davenport when, after Kellar had told William that Kellar couldn't put a pet monkey and dog into the passenger car of the train, and William had told Kellar *"You do as I tell you Harry. You are my servant"*.

It wasn't just Kellar that William Davenport had rubbed up the wrong way, as Fay, the third performer in the 'Davenport Brothers and Fay' walked away with Kellar.

Kellar and Fay set off to the Southern States and down through Mexico and South America, performing a version of the 'spirit medium' act that they had been working with the Davenports, until they eventually parted ways, having lost most of their earnings for the tour in a shipwreck. Fay went back to the Davenports and Keller headed across the Atlantic to London.

Here he made his way to the Egyptian Hall. The Egyptian Hall had been built many years earlier in 1812, and had been the first Egyptian style building built in England. To start with it had been a museum for a collection owned by a collector named William Bullock, and had hosted magical performances since shortly before Victoria came to the throne.

In 1873 the management of the Hall fell to theatre manager William Morton, who brought in a pair of illusionists, Maskelyne and Cook, who took a room on the first floor holding just under 300 people, and referred to it as 'England's Home of Mystery', hoping that they could run shows there for three months. In the end, it ran for thirty years.

When Kellar saw the Egyptian Hall, he was both impressed by the idea of performing in a single theatre, and by some of the illusions he saw performed by a magician named Buatier de Kolta, from whom Kellar purchased a 'vanishing birdcage illusion'.

Over the next few years Keller toured around the world, but he never let go of the thought of having a 'home' theatre to perform at, and in 1884, at the age of 35, he opened his own 'Egyptian Hall', an old masonic temple in

Philadelphia, and performed there for 264 performances before he decided it was time to get back on the road and went off on tour again.

He repeated this again in 1891, opening his second 'Egyptian Hall' on the same street as the first (the first having burned down shortly after the end of his first run), and this time stayed for another seven months before he went off on tour once again.

There are descriptions of his charming nature and the twinkle in his eyes which made audiences love him. There is even speculation, quite likely correct, that he was the inspiration for the 'Wizard of Oz' in L. Frank Baum's books.

He kept touring and bringing magic to people until 1908, when he retired from the stage and handed over his mantle to a young magician named Howard Thurston, who would go on to be a big name in magic himself.

Much like I did with Robert-Houdin, I am going to end my discussion of Kellar by telling you about a time he came out of retirement, although this is a far more heart-warming story.

In 1917, during the First World War, Harry Houdini was putting on a show with the Society of American Magicians to raise money to support the family of American sailors killed when their ship was sunk by a German U-boat.

Houdini managed to persuade Kellar to come out of retirement for one last show, and not just any show, but the Hippodrome in New York, the biggest theatre in the world at the time.

Kellar performed his act, and then prepared to leave the stage, but that wasn't good enough for the great Harry Kellar, not if Houdini had anything to do with it.

Houdini came onstage and announced that, *"America's greatest magician should be carried off in triumph after his final public performance."*

This is exactly what happened. A Sedan chair was brought onto the stage, and with Kellar safely sat in it he was raised into the air by members of the Society of American Magicians, and, as the orchestra played 'Auld Lang Syne', Kellar was paraded off from the stage, a fitting ending to the final show performed by *"the most beloved magician in history"*.

Madame Adelaide Hermann – The Queen of Magic
(1853–1932)

In case you haven't figured it out yet, the vast majority of names mentioned in the book so far have one thing in common. They are all men.

This, sadly, isn't because I have set out to write a book that excludes female magicians but rather because the history of magic is, by and large, a history of men.

It seems unbelievable in some ways that in the United Kingdom, women were given the vote on the same terms as men in this country in 1928, but it wasn't until 1991, over sixty years later, that women were allowed to join the Magic Circle, and then it wasn't a unanimous decision, but in fact, only seventy-five per cent of members voted to let women in. That is a clear majority, but it still feels like that number should have been a hundred per cent.

By the time we get to 2016, twenty-five years after women were allowed in, according to a blog post on the website of female magician and mentalist Katherine Mills, of one thousand five hundred members of the Magic Circle, only sixty-eight were women. That is less than five per cent of the total membership.

As someone (who, exactly, seems to be under some debate) once famously said, "There are lies, damned lies, and then there are statistics."

I've already given my reasons earlier in the book for not being a member of the Magic Circle, and there may be plenty of reasons why female magicians may not want to join, especially while it is still a male-dominated club, which is really something for the Magic Circle itself to find a solution to, and it doesn't necessarily mean that less than five per cent of all magicians are female today.

Having a look at 'The Magician's Podcast', in which Richard Young tried to interview prominent magicians, and I know he made an effort to talk to a range of different magicians, only seven out of one hundred magicians interviewed were female, while an article I found on 'inews' in 2019 tells us that *in the US, around 93 per cent of the Academy of Magical Arts' magician-level members are male*.

It seems that this figure of five to seven per cent is a fair estimate of the percentage of female magicians as we come to the end of the second decade of the twenty-first century, and just from the anecdotal evidence of the young people who come up to me and tell me that they want to be magicians, or want to show me a trick, they are overwhelmingly young men.

However, in the history of magic there is one name that stands out, and allows me to bring a female magician into this chapter, that of Madame Adelaide Hermann – The Queen of Magic.

Hermann started out the same as most women in magic at that time, training in dance and acrobatics, and then moving into magic as a magician's assistant, in her case assisting her husband, Alexander Hermann, or 'Hermann the Great', a French-born magician who, by the time he married Adelaide, had already performed a three year run at the Egyptian Hall, and toured shows around the capitals of Europe.

The pair got to know each other on a boat heading for America in 1874 having met before while they were in London, and by the time they docked in New York it was only a matter of time until Adelaide Scarcez would become Adelaide Herrmann, which happened the following year when they were married by the Mayor of New York.

The pair toured together, and Adelaide moved from being an assistant to being a big part of the show, and in 1888 the pair put a show together to expose the methods of a particularly nasty, fraudulent medium, Ann O'Delia Diss Debar, who, at one time spent seven years in prison for obtaining property under false pretences and other far more serious crimes. In this act of exposing her methods, both of the Herrmanns showed themselves not just to be skilled magicians, but also people who were willing to stand up on the right side of the schism that was opening up between magicians dealing with the Spiritualist ideas at the time.

More on that in a later chapter.

Alexander Herrmann passed away in 1896 and Adelaide was faced with a decision whether or not to continue with their magic show. For three seasons she worked with Alexander's nephew, but it didn't work out.

So Adelaide made the decision to tour alone, and what a marvellous choice that was for magic!

She gained huge amounts of success touring on her own, earning her the title 'The Queen of Magic'. She managed over twenty-five years as a headline performer, and in 1903 she made her Broadway debut.

There was nothing about her act that was compromised by her sex, she even performed a bullet catch within her act, an effect that had killed a number of performers who had attempted it.

It is a shame that, over ninety years after her death, women are still massively under-represented in the world of magic.

Adelaide Herrmann did have something very important to say, at a time when headlines were announcing her as 'the world's only woman magician'.

"I shall not be content until I am recognized by the public as a leader in my profession, and entirely irrespective of the question of sex."

Although this section has discussed women in magic, I think that there can be no doubt that she succeeded in her goal.

Any magician who spends twenty-five years headlining tours, including visits to Broadway, deserves their place as one of the top performers in our profession.

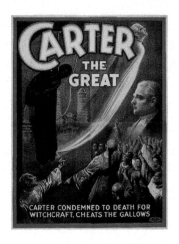

Carter The Great
1874-1936

It is always a bold choice for a performer to choose a stage name which features words like 'The Great', or 'The Amazing', because once you make that claim, you have to live up to it. There are some magicians, such as 'The Amazing Randy', who can absolutely live up to their name, while there are others (and I shall certainly not be naming any names here) who have adopted these titles without being able to back them up.

Carter the Great, or Charles Joseph Carter, is one of those magicians for whom the title is well deserved.

I first came across the name, 'Carter the Great' in a fictionalised version of his life, 'Carter Beats The Devil' by Glen David Gold, which is a fantastic read if you enjoy this period in the history of magic.

Although Carter got into magic at a young age, he was clever enough not to leap to the title of 'the Great', instead he went with 'Master Charles Carter the Original Boy Magician.' This, however, was a bit of a mouthful, and probably not easy to fit on a poster, and so he quickly just became 'Master Charles Carter the Magician'.

Carter toured his shows across America until the turn of the century, adding first a wife, who joined the show, and then a son, Laurence, to his entourage as they took the magic from place to place, and he still hadn't added 'the Great' to his billing.

By the start of the Twentieth Century, however, the family had become tired of life on the road, and stopped their tour in Chicago and Carter started his own entertainment agency, 'The National Theatrical Exchange' and a magazine, 'The Chicago Footlights'.

I have learned from writing this book just how much time writing can take up, and how long the process can take, and so the combination of producing a magazine while running a successful agency sounds like it would take up every minute that Carter had, and yet during this period of time he also managed to attend and graduate Law School.

In 1907, 'Carter the Great', for now that appeared on his posters, set off with his family on a world tour that would take him as far as Australia, India and Egypt, with many more stops as he travelled around. With heavy equipment, and no air travel available to get around quickly, this meant the equipment was loaded on and off ships.

At one point, while he was planning to return to the USA in 1912, he could not board the steamship he wanted because they did not have space available for all of his equipment. This must have been frustrating for him as the ship was certainly big enough, but he could not get on board that particular ship, and so had to stay in England as the Titanic set off for America without him.

In 1917, Carter tried his hand at running a magic shop, and purchased the Markinta Magic Shop. The Markinta brand is still going today, and the shop was famous for being the place where the Society of American Magicians was founded.

The store didn't do very well under Carter's ownership however, and one anecdote has a suggestion why. The story goes that Carter would keep his pet lion, Monty, in the back of the shop, and for some reason, when the lion roared, customers would hurriedly make their way out of the shop.

In 1936, on a boat to India to perform over there, Charles Carter suffered a heart attack, and his son Larry, who had toured with Carter since he was a baby, took over the show, and took on the mantle of Carter the Great for a short time, before leaving showbusiness to sell cars.

Charles Carter never fully recovered, and died of a second heart attack in Bombay shortly after on the 13th February.

The Dangerous Side of Magic

Magic is all about illusion, and sometimes you may see magicians performing feats which seem incredibly dangerous. One of my all-time favourite examples is when the magicians Penn and Teller performed an extraordinary television stunt involving driving a massive lorry with its wheels rolling right over Teller – with a beautiful twist ending which I will leave you to discover yourself by watching it. However, when performed properly (and the Penn and Teller trick certainly was), there should be no real danger of serious injury to the performer; the illusion is what magic is (or should be, in my opinion) all about.

There are, however, many magicians over the years whose magic hasn't held to this ideal and who have performed magic which has the potential, if something goes wrong, to cause serious injury or even, in extreme cases, death.

In this chapter, I am going to share with you a handful of the stories from the history of magic of where things did go wrong, with tragic results.

Let this be a reminder to all budding magicians that a trick which appears dangerous can sometimes bring in a crowd but that you owe it to yourself and to your audience to minimise any risks.

Hopefully these stories will also have more practical advice for those of you too sensible to risk real danger.

We will begin with Chung Ling Soo, who you will remember was not actually the Chinese immigrant that he pretended to be on stage, but a Scottish gentleman by the name of William Ellsworth Robinson.

I think the moral of this story will be to always check your props, a lesson which I have learned the hard way from forgetting to reset tricks following a show, and then halfway through the next performance realising that the piece I need to make a trick work is still in the pocket of my close-up bag in the wings.

Robinson, sadly, didn't get a chance to learn from his mistake when his bullet catch trick went wrong.

The trick was revealed at the inquest following his death, where it was explained that Robinson had become lazy when removing the bullets (never actually fired) from the gun after the trick, and so gunpowder residue had built up inside the barrel. That night, instead of bypassing the main barrel and firing off a blank, the flash from the firing had ignited the residue and fired the real bullet into Robinson's chest.

For the first time on stage he broke the character of Chung Ling Soo, and much to the surprise of his audience, he spoke English, saying, *"Oh my God. Something's happened. Lower the curtain."*

Robinson was rushed to hospital but had died from his wounds by the following morning.

Our second unfortunate tale comes with the warning to always thoroughly rehearse your tricks, and make sure you have timed them correctly, especially where there is risk involved.

When Karr the Magician, whose real name was Charles Rowen, attempted to escape from a straitjacket in South Africa in1930, he decided to add to the excitement of the event by having a car drive straight towards him from two hundred yards away, accelerating to a speed of forty-five miles an hour, giving Rowen just fifteen seconds to make his escape. To cut a rather gory story short, Rowen failed to make the escape in time. To his credit, before he died, he made it clear that the driver was not at fault in any way.

I think the third tale will reiterate the message to check your props, but in particular, to be sure to check anything that has been through a transport system to ensure it has not been damaged en route.

Royden Joseph Gilbert Raison de la Genesta was at a theatre in Kentucky, also in 1930, when he attempted to copy the milk can escape made famous by Harry Houdini (and you can see a picture of Houdini preparing for this stunt in the next chapter).

The idea of the escape is that a milk can, just large enough to hold a person, is filled with water. The escape artist then climbs inside at which point the lid is secured and the can is hidden by a curtain or screen. Several minutes later, the magician bursts through the curtain, soaking wet, but safe.

Unfortunately, on the fateful day in Kentucky, Genesta had not realised that the milk can had been dented while being transported to the venue, in such a way that it made the escape impossible.

We're going to head back to the 'Bullet Catch' trick, for a lesson in dealing with participants. As mentioned, in the card trick taught in the playing card chapter, the reason I get a participant to show the rest of the audience is to protect myself against the participant deliberately (by lying about the card) or accidentally (by forgetting the card) ruining the conclusion of the trick. You can imagine, therefore, that I certainly wouldn't recommend putting your life into the hands of a participant during any trick.

Unfortunately, in 1820, the Polish magician Madame DeLinsky took to the stage to catch not one, but six bullets in her teeth, in front of a German Prince.

Six soldiers were brought in as participants in the trick, their job being to fire their guns at Madame Delinsky, having been secretly instructed beforehand to only load blanks in the guns.

It only took one soldier, whether through nerves, misunderstanding or forgetfulness to load a live bullet instead of a blank, and Delinsky became another victim of the bullet catch, a trick which has killed at least twelve performers who were attempting it.

The final lesson in this chapter, is to have respect for the audience whenever you decide to perform a dangerous effect and know the impact that something happening to you could have on them.

It was Halloween, 1987, and a magician presented a live special on BBC television. The audience were warned in advance that if they were of a nervous disposition that they should turn off before the final effect of the show.

Millions of viewers were watching as the magician, Paul Daniels, was strapped into an iron maiden, a large metal box filled with spikes. Daniels showed how the effect would work.

He was to be strapped inside, with manacles locked around his wrist, and a metal collar locked around his neck. If he couldn't get out in time, the door of the iron maiden would slam shut, driving its spikes into him.

Once he was locked in, the trick began, and then the door slammed shut before Daniels had got out.

The lights went down, the show immediately cut to the credits, and you could hear the live studio audience being asked to leave the building.

People were horrified to see this on television, and over a thousand people got on the phone straight away to find out whether Daniels was alright, and many people I speak to still have this memory burned in their minds.

I suppose there is one more lesson to take away from this chapter… Sometimes magicians will decide to trick you.

While all of the other stories in this chapter are true stories of tricks which went wrong leading to the deaths, this trick had gone exactly as it was intended to go, it was, after all, a magic show. They may have underestimated, however, the reaction of the audience.

In the end, Daniels had to make an extra appearance that night to let people know he was alright, and even to write a letter to 'The Times' newspaper to defend himself and the choice to end the show in the way he had.

"The last trick on the Hallowe'en Show has received a general criticism from the Press of being in bad taste but, of course, good or bad taste is a very subjective area.

After all, good taste is only the material or opinion that agrees with your own. It was Hallowe'en and I decided to present a piece of black theatre to create suspense and horror for the viewers, much in the style of Orson Welles when, in the 1930s, he activated the nation with his radio version of 'War of the Worlds'. Putting bad taste into my magical world would, I suppose, be doing a crucifix escape on the Easter show, but something macabre on Hallowe'en I think fitted the bill perfectly."

This brings us back around to the beginning of the chapter, because if that was the reaction of people to seeing a faked death, then imagine how much worse it would have affected the audience had it been real.

For the record, I agree with Paul Daniels about finishing his show like this on a Halloween show, the ending was fitting and he performed the trick in a way that was perfectly safe. I'm not advocating against using magic and theatre to create dangerous-looking tricks – I have, after all, performed an escape from in front of a Steam Roller and spent many years juggling knives, axes and mantraps. I knew, however, that I had thoroughly prepared these stunts, and had plenty of safety measures in place.

This takes me right round to my initial thought, if you want to do a trick that appears dangerous, you owe it to your audience to make sure that the danger is merely theatrical, and that they are not going to have to live with seeing you seriously injured or killed.

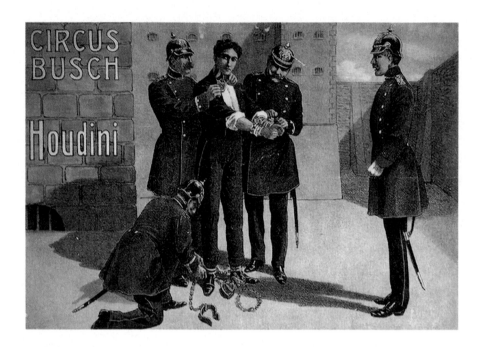

Houdini

If you ask anyone to name a magician from history, and for many people just to name any magician, the name most likely to come up is Houdini. I admit, I haven't tested this scientifically, but I did a quick 'straw poll' on Instagram and Twitter and found that over half the people named Houdini (and that those people who said a different name were, in the majority, magicians, many of whom picked great magicians who would, however, likely be a lot less familiar outside of those working in the art).

I am not going to even begin to attempt to tell Houdini's life story here, not only are there far too many stories to tell, but I think that his biography has already been written up perfectly by Sid Fleischman in his book 'Escape! The Story of the Great Houdini', which I strongly recommend.

This leaves me free to share one of my favourite stories from Houdini's life.

For those of you unfamiliar with Harry Houdini, or those with only a passing knowledge of his name, you may know that Harry Houdini was an American magician famous for performances of daring escapes around the turn of the century from the 18th to the 19th Century.

That, at least, is what Houdini would have wanted you to think, and indeed in September 1919, he filled out a passport application which he completed and signed as to the truth of the following statements (words in bold are those that Houdini wrote on the form):

*"I, **Harry Houdini**, a native and loyal citizen of the United States, hereby apply to the Department of State, at Washington, for a passport.*

*I solemnly swear that I was born at **Appleton, Wis**, in the State of **Wis**, on or about the 6th day of **April 1874**."*

As an official document and such an important form as one used to obtain a passport (which you can see on the next page, thanks to the National Archives), you may have thought that Houdini would have been careful to have the correct information. You may have thought that, but you would have been wrong because there are three changes here from when Harry was born.

The first is perfectly acceptable, as although Harry Houdini was not his name at birth (which was Erich

Weisz), it was the name he used for his performances and is the name he was known as to millions of people around the world and in 1913 he had legally changed his name to Harry Houdini.

What is difficult to excuse, however, is his 'solemnly swearing' that he was born in the town of Appleton in the state of Wisconsin and his claim to be a native of the United States. Houdini was, in fact, born in Budapest in the (then) Kingdom of Hungary – which a quick look on Google Maps tells me is approximately 4,700 miles away. This wasn't a small fact to get wrong – imagine the result if you were filling in a passport form today and you claimed to have been born not only in a different country but in a different continent from where you had actually been born.

The other misinformation that Houdini recorded in this form was that he was born on the 6th of April 1874, whereas he had, in fact, been born on the 24th of March 1874. This, to me, seems the strangest of these three statements. The use of his preferred name is, I think, completely fair. I can also understand why he might want to simplify things by claiming to be a native of the United States rather than complicating matters by putting down that he had come to the United States from Hungary with his mother and siblings when he was just four years old, from which time he did grow up in Appleton.

The question of Houdini's moving birthday, and at some points in his earlier life, his birth year, may come down to confusion and the fact that Harry himself wasn't sure, as the exact record of his birth was lost.

I don't point out all of these minor untruths about Houdini in order to bring him down, but rather to introduce you to the idea that Harry Houdini was a creation designed by the magician himself, as he was always a master of self-publicity, and would weave stories around himself that caught the public attention, and that was part of his magic.

I spoke, when talking about Carter the Great, about the boldness of choosing titles. Harry Houdini was bold enough to give himself titles and even when he was starting out as a card magician, he had to be Harry Houdini, King of Cards.

Houdini experts still debate whether certain stories of him are true or false, but I think that some of the stories can be both.

I think that one of the biggest reasons that Houdini, nearly a full century after his death, remains the most famous magician in the world is that other magicians, for all their skill and all the joy they bring, are still real people.

Harry Houdini has surpassed that. Harry Houdini has become a legend, and a legend of his own making.

I will share my favourite Houdini story here, and, in the spirit of history I will hint at why they may not be entirely true. For much of the rest of this chapter, however, I shall remove my historian hat, and replace it with my storytelling hat reserved for legends[33].

The most famous of the Houdini legends, immortalised in both the 1953 film 'Houdini' and the mini-series of the same name from 2014, as well as in countless books and articles, and told by Houdini himself, took place when he jumped off a bridge in Detroit on Christmas Day in 1906. Or possibly in Detroit on 27th November 1906. Or possibly in Pittsburgh. He couldn't quite keep the story straight.

Houdini certainly did carry out 'bridge jump' escapes, in which he would be handcuffed and wrapped in chains before leaping from a bridge and into a river to complete his escape. This type of publicity stunt would draw vast crowds and was a great way to increase ticket sales for his upcoming shows.

---

[33] Its bigger, bright blue, and has flashing lights, in case you are wondering, and is, of course, legendary.

He did have trouble in Dresden, Germany in 1900 when the police tried to stop him from making the jump, but there were no laws they could use to prevent him doing so.

Houdini made the jump that day in Dresden, and made his escape, emerging triumphantly and swimming over to the grassy banks of the river to climb out. Here he was met by the Dresden police, who immediately arrested him.

What was his crime?

It was illegal to walk on the grass!

Now we can return to that fateful November (or December) day in Detroit (or Pittsburgh) in1906. Harry had prepared himself to make his jump.

In his own description of that day, from a 'Washington Post' article in 1912, the earliest I have seen a mention of it:

"At Belle Bridge, Detroit, my foolhardiness nearly cost me my life. It was on Christmas Day, 1906. The river was frozen. A circular hole was cut about six feet in diameter, and into this I dived. But what a struggle I had getting out again. I shall bear the scars of that experience to my dying day."

Records show that Houdini did make a jump from Belle Bridge, but in November, and at a time when there was no ice reported at all. I think I have now done my due diligence with the history side of things, and it is time to tell the legend.

On that day in 1906, Houdini was prepared to make a leap from the bridge. When he and his team arrived at the bridge, however, they noticed a major problem with performing the stunt that day.

"Nature was unkind, however, and when the day came the river had been frozen over to a depth of seven inches, which, as a matter of fact, wasn't surprising, as it was midwinter. But ice-water never has had any terrors for me, and a hole was cut in the ice just below the bridge and everybody, including a crowd of several thousand of persons, arrived on time."

With the hole cut in the ice, and the 'crowd of several thousand' watching, Houdini made the leap through the hole in the ice, and into the icy water below. The cold struck him, and shocked him for a moment, but Houdini had trained himself to hold his breath in icy water, and the shock passed almost immediately, allowing him to get on with the task of freeing himself from the chains and manacles that restrained him.

This would be no problem for the 'King of Handcuffs' as he now called himself, and he made short work of his restraints, so now all he had to do was to wait a little longer to allow the suspense to build up on the surface, and then rise to the surface and to the applause of the waiting crowds, another successful escape.

It was as he began to make his way to the surface that Houdini realised his mistake. While he had been focused on the handcuffs and chains, he had not realised that the river's current had been pulling him downstream, away from the hole in the ice. In the murky gloom under the water, he couldn't even make out where the hole was.

This time, Houdini knew he was really in trouble. Though he had trained himself to hold his breath for extended periods of time, he was running short, and needed to get to the surface now. Even the greatest escapologist in the world would not be able to break through seven inches of ice before his air ran out and so he had to find the hole.

He looked around, hoping to see beams of light coming down through the hole, but there was no clue to be seen.

Houdini knew that he had to stay calm, that panic would mean certain death, but his lungs were starting to ache with the need for breath. Then, he found his salvation.

"I found an air pocket, a space in which the ice seemed to curve upward, leaving an inch or more of room between the surface of the water and the ice above. I lay flat on my back, tight up against the ice, and breathed."

While the supply of air was short, and cold water slipped into his mouth along with his breaths, Houdini had oxygen again, enough to allow him a moment to think, and to figure out a way to make his escape. Perhaps, in this pocket of air, the upward slope of the ice meant that it was thinner at this point.

Houdini still had, in his hand, one of the manacles that had restrained him, and realised that this was the only tool available. He couldn't smash through the ice, but maybe, just maybe, he could cut through it.

He placed the sharpest corner of the manacle against the ice, and began to rotate his body to bring that point in a circle, like a jewel thief cutting through glass. It took time and patience, and he would not have made it without the air pocket, but all of a sudden the circle of ice gave way to produce a hole. He had survived!

"Suddenly I bobbed up through the hole, and the men reached down and lifted me out onto the ice, wrapped me up and hurried me to my hotel.

The crowd that had come to see me and my assistants believed that I had been drowned and, although I didn't hear it, they say that a mighty cheer went up when I appeared."

Houdini told this story many times, and with many slight variations, and the story spread and became a legend.

So, whether it was Detroit or Pittsburgh, November or December, truth, lies or exaggeration didn't really matter in the grand scheme of things. What really mattered was that, once again, Houdini had crossed into the pages of legend.

Magicians among the Spirits

For several years I toured a show called 'The Non-Psychic 'Psychic' Show', which was in part inspired by the film which first got me into performing escapology. The film is 'Death Defying Acts' with Guy Pearce, Catherine Zeta-Jones and Saoirse Ronan, and, while it leaves a lot to be desired in terms of historical accuracy regarding Houdini's life,[34] it is still an interesting watch and is a window into some of the ideas behind Houdini's search later in his life for someone who could truly contact the dead, and his personal mission to expose fraudulent mediums.

One of my great joys when touring 'The Non-Psychic 'Psychic' Show' was that some modern 'psychic mediums'

---

[34] Which, as discussed in the chapter before, is equally true of Houdini himself.

would come to the show, and discuss it with me afterwards (although I am aware that some complained about the show, and at one theatre I was told that a 'psychic' who performs in theatres had refused to go on within a month of my show, which I found interesting).

The reason, I think, that people claiming psychic powers could come along and enjoy my show was the statement I made at the beginning of the performance. I knew each night in the audience that there would be people who absolutely believed in psychics, people who absolutely didn't believe in psychics, and those who don't know one way or another.[35] It doesn't matter which of those categories you fall into because my show (and this chapter) doesn't set out to prove whether psychics exist.

What we know for a fact is that at least some of those people claiming psychic powers are frauds, and until we take those people out of the equation we can't even begin to discuss whether or not psychic powers actually exist, and what might cause them.

In my chapter on Victorian Magicians, I talked about a schism opening between magicians over the subject of spiritualism. On the one hand, you had people like the Herrmanns, who produced their show exposing the secrets of the fraudulent medium and all-round horrendous person

---

[35] 'I don't know', by the way, is a perfectly good response, and the one which I fall into on this subject, as with many others. 'I don't know' doesn't mean you give both sides equal weight, but you are still prepared to accept evidence in both directions. Politics and the pandemic seem to have made everything more and more binary over the past few years, and perhaps it would be a better world if we all learned to say 'I don't know' a little more often.

Ann O'Delia Diss Debar, while on the other hand you had people who took to the stage to use magician's tricks in order to pretend to have these powers themselves, which continues today.

Why does it matter? What if the mediums are just providing comfort to dead relatives?

These are questions I have heard asked, and the answer is subjective. It matters if someone is deliberately perpetrating fraud, and telling people they have received messages from dead friends and relatives which the medium has made up, as this distorts the true memory of the person they are grieving over. To make money out of people's grief by conning them into thinking that you are their only link to the deceased is morally abhorrent, and I hope, whether you believe psychics are real or not, that you would agree that this is the case with any fraudulent medium.

It gets even more serious when these psychics go on to get involved in things like police investigations, when the information that they are giving is wrong. One of the most famous examples of a medium getting involved in criminal investigations, and I am not saying that she was or wasn't fraudulent[36], just that she was wrong, was Sylvia Browne.

She would go on television shows and talk to the parents of missing children on air. In 2008 the British television standards agency Ofcom sanctioned ITV2 for showing an

---

[36] Although she did plead 'No Contest' alongside her husband when the pair faced felony charges over fraudulently selling securities in California.

episode of 'The Montel Williams Show' from 2002. The reason that they faced those sanctions was a segment with Sylvia Browne, in which she told the parents of missing eleven year old boy Shawn Hornbeck that he had been kidnapped in a blue sedan by a dark-skinned, Hispanic man, with long dreadlocks, and was in a wooded area within twenty miles of their house. When the parents asked Browne whether their son was 'still with us', she told them 'no'.

Shawn Hornbeck was eventually found, alive, in 2007 after his kidnapper was picked up for another kidnapping. The kidnapper had been driving a truck, not a sedan, and was a short-haired, white man.

In case you think I am cherry-picking a case when she was egregiously wrong, a study by the 'Skeptical Inquirer' in 2010 looked into Sylvia Browne's claim that she was eighty-five per cent correct in her predictions. The study looked at all 115 cases that she had given predictions for, and looked at how many cases she was correct in. The findings were quite clear. Of the twenty-five cases in which the outcome is known, Brown was correct zero times. She was wrong in all twenty-five cases, on multiple occasions telling the families of missing children that they were dead when they were not, or that they were alive when that was not true.

I hope that this gives another indication of why it is important to ascertain whether someone is using magical methods, such as cold-reading, to fake psychic powers.

Even Houdini, as a young performer before he found fame, spent a period of time with his wife Bess performing a medium act, and gave it up due to guilt at what he was doing. He used techniques that other fake psychics have and probably still do use, such as arriving in a town and visiting a local graveyard to note some names of the recently deceased, and then visiting a local library to look through newspapers to find obituaries and reports of deaths[37].

He would express regret for doing the act later in his life when, after his mother died, he tried to find a medium who could contact her. Having found that all of the mediums he visited were using magicians' methods that he saw through easily, he began a campaign about the fraudulent mediums and wrote about this in his book 'A Magician among the Spirits'.

Some of Houdini's investigations (and these are the truth rather than some of his 'legends' as in the previous chapter) have an air of a Bugs Bunny cartoon about them, as he would go into seances around the world, and apply little tests to ascertain what would happen during the complete blackness of a seance room.[38]

When he visited the séance room of George Rannan, for example, he got to witness first-hand how, after the lights were out, ghostly voices would emanate from a

---

[37] Obviously, for the modern day fraud, this is made significantly easier owing to the access available to much of this information and more online.

[38] Which is, by the way, cheating. All magic would be considerably easier if the audience were just to accept that we would do it in complete darkness, and that they would just have to trust what the magician was saying.

megaphone with no one speaking into it. Then the rest of the people in the room got to witness, after the lights came back on, the black smudge around Rannan's mouth from the boot polish that Houdini had applied to the mouthpiece of the megaphone when he had been allowed to examine it beforehand.

There was also the case of a medium from London who claimed he could make the ghost of Dante, a barefooted ghost of the writer of 'The Divine Comedy'. Exactly why the ghost of Dante would choose to appear seven hundred and fifty miles from where he died, or why there was a shortage of shoes in Heaven were never quite explained. It was a big surprise one night, therefore, when Houdini saw that someone had accidentally scattered tacks over the floor, and it appeared that a supernatural entity can still be hurt by a tack in the foot.

Unfortunately, despite all that Houdini did, there were some who still would not believe that these people were frauds, and even more than that, believed that Houdini was lying about his own magic powers, that he was really using genuine magic and claiming it as tricks.

His friendship with Sir Arthur Conan Doyle suffered, as Doyle was a staunch believer, and even arranged for his wife, and medium, to arrange a sitting with Houdini. The medium on that occasion produced fifteen pages of 'automatic writing', claiming that the spirit of Harry's mother had controlled her hand. A cross on the top of the page (Harry's mother was Jewish), the fact that she addressed the letter to Harry (his mother had only ever called him Erich) and that she wrote in English (a language which his mother never spoke) was all the proof that Harry needed that no contact had been made, especially when he found out later that Lady Doyle had spoken with Bess, Harry's wife, and gathered during that conversation most of the details revealed in the letter.

One of the saddest examples of people not quite understanding that Houdini performed tricks, however, was in the opening of his book about his time investigating the mediums.

"A memorable incident in my life and one that shows how little the world at large understands the methods by which my mysteries are produced and also shows how easy it is for even a great intellect, faced with a mystery it cannot fathom, to conclude that there is something supernatural involved, has to do with Madame Sarah Bernhardt.

During one of my various engagements in Paris she had witnessed my performances and was anxious to see one of my outdoor exploits, so, when we were both playing at the same time in Boston, out of good camaraderie I gave a special performance at my hotel adding a few extra experiments for her benefit. As we were seated in the motor car on the way to my demonstration she placed her arm gently around my shoulder, and in that wonderful speaking voice with which she was gifted and which has thrilled thousands of auditors, but now stilled forever, she said to me:

"Houdini, you do such marvellous things. Couldn't you—could you bring back my leg for me?"

I looked at her, startled, and failing to see any mischievous sparkle in her eye replied: "Good heavens, Madame, certainly not; you cannot be serious. You know my powers are limited and you are actually asking me to do the impossible."

"Yes," she said as she leaned closer to me, "but you do the impossible."

This is the difficult line that an honest magician has to tread, how far do you allow audiences to believe in magic, and that has to be a personal answer for each person.

On the other side of the schism created by the rising spiritualist movement, there were magicians who took to the stage to perform shows based upon the techniques that some of the frauds would use, leaving the audiences to assume that they had true powers, and the most famous of these were Ira and William, the Davenport Brothers.

The Spiritualist movement in America had its origins in the late 1840s, when two young girls, The Fox Sisters, were found to be able to receive messages from the deceased through a series of mysterious rapping noises, which the older of the pair confessed, in 1888, they had learned to make by cracking the knuckles in their toes. A confession from Margaret, denied by her sister Catherine, was not enough to deter either believer or those who made their money from exploiting their beliefs.

Seances often happened in people's homes, in darkened rooms. A far cry from people like Sylvia Browne in the modern era who mostly use words and talking as their tools of the trade. Modern fraudulent psychics are generally adept at 'cold-reading', a technique that allows someone to sound like they are making incredibly accurate statements without any prior knowledge, or 'hot-reading', which involves them revealing information they have learned through research, or details you have given them through your appearance or things they can see around you.

Seances in the era of the Davenports, however, were altogether a more theatrical affair! Banging drums, spirit writing on slates, and even spirit hands and ectoplasm appearing, this was a full-on experience, and this was what the brothers chose as the basis of their act.

I myself have performed a number of séance style effects onstage, the theatricality behind them can be great fun to explore, and I have even performed my own smaller, comedy version of the 'spirit cabinet' routine that made the Davenport Brothers famous, so I certainly don't take issue with them wanting to take these elements of the séances and applying them to the stage. The problem I have with them is that they claimed that their performances were true demonstrations of the supernatural, even going so far as to have a former minister, and now spiritualist, Dr. J. B. Ferguson introducing their shows who specifically presented the brothers as users of 'spirit power', and not magic effects.

Personally, some of the tricks I did in my version of the spirit cabinet were fairly difficult – so I'm certainly not about to let a bunch of spirits take the credit!

Cosmic Xposure

The spirit cabinet routine, the one which made them famous, involved a large wooden cabinet, raised from the stage, which you can see in the photograph that started this chapter. The brothers would allow people to inspect the cabinet, to make sure there was nobody hidden inside, and then the brothers would take up their positions on chairs at either end inside the cabinet.

Lengths of rope were then used to restrain the two brothers so that they couldn't move from the chairs, or use their hands in any way, and then the doors to the cabinet were closed and the audience waited.
As you can see from the image below, this is when chaos would occur. Tambourines would rattle, megaphones would call out ghostly messages, and objects would fly

from inside the cabinet to all corners of the stage[39]. This caused a sensation with people flocking to the theatres in the belief that there were true spirits at work.

The magicians who believed that it was wrong to use magic methods to gain followers who believed they were using supernatural means in their shows (which traces back at least to 'The Discoverie of Witchcraft' and continues to the modern day), made an effort to show the public that this wasn't the case, including many of the people we have already discussed.

John Nevil Maskelyne and George Alfred Cooke, who you may remember as the men who started a three month run and stayed for thirty years, were affronted when they saw

[39] If you want to see a modern interpretation of the spirit cabinet, then I can strongly recommend watching Derren Brown's 'Séance' special, a thoroughly entertaining show which includes his version of the effect.

the trick being performed as though it were for real, and recreated the spirit cabinet, revealing the Davenports as frauds in a show in 1865. Robert-Houdin also performed duplicate effects, and made it clear that they were being performed through natural means, and Herrmann the Great, husband of Adelaide Herrmann, wrote an article for 'Cosmopolitan Magazine' about the brothers, including that the night he was there a group of college students had brought lights to turn on during one of the blackouts, catching the Davenport Brothers free from the cabinet and playing with instruments on either side of the stage.

This divide between magicians, and those who would corrupt the art to deceive grieving people continues today.

I hope anyone reading this book who gets into magic will be on the right side of this schism.

Sawing A Woman In Half

I mentioned in my 'overture' at the start of this book that I might delve into some of my thoughts and philosophies regarding the 'magician's assistant', and as we move to what is arguably one of the two most recognised, and most clichéd tricks performed by magicians, alongside pulling a rabbit out of a hat.

On the 17th of January 1921, at the Finsbury Park Empire in London, a magician named P.T. Selbit earned his place in the history of magic when he performed the first public performance of this trick, a trick which a little over a century later means that still, a good number of times a year, I am asked whether I'm going to saw someone's wife in half (probably only topped by the number of times I'm asked to make someone's husband disappear).

I, personally, have never sawn a woman into halves, nor
have I actually ever seen this particular trick performed
live (although I have seen many versions on television
over the years), and it is not an effect that I am ever likely
to put in my act, mainly because of my personal opinions
on the subject of magician's assistants.

My biggest problem with the role of the magician's
assistant, aside from the fact that historically the assistant
was almost always female, and the magician male, is the
amount of skill that the assistant must possess. In illusions,
this can often mean that the assistant is actually doing
almost all of the work, while the magician is just standing
around the box waving their hands around and acting all
'magical'.

One beautifully put together counter to this was 'The Great
Tomsoni and Company', a double act of Johnny
Thompson and his wife, Pamela Hayes. In their act
together, Johnny (as The Great Tomsoni) would perform
the magic, while Pamela played a gum chewing assistant
who seemed to want nothing less than to assist the
magician, in a masterpiece of a comedy magic routine.

This aside, if there is a need for two people in the act, I
would rather that, like the comedy illusionist double-act
'Young and Strange', consisting of magicians Richard
Young and Sam Strange, which allows them to share both
the traditional magician and assistant roles throughout their
act, including the best version of the 'sticks through
cardboard box illusion', in which Young is put into a
cardboard box through which Strange then thrusts large

numbers of long wooden poles through the box. I have seen similar effects with magicians and assistants, using swords, broomsticks, and even umbrellas, but the more equal power dynamic of two magicians performing the act together is one I much prefer.

I have always had the rule in my show that anything which appears dangerous or embarrassing should be done to me, and not to another person. Enough of my views on this, let us return to the first version of sawing a woman in half.

P. T. Selbit was born Percy Thomas Tibbles in London in 1881, and while he was apprenticed to a silversmith in his youth he would take the opportunity to sneak down to the workshop of a magician and creator of magical effects, Charles Morritt, which was housed in the basement of the silversmith's shop.

He would go on to become a magician, creating his stage name of P.T. Selbit simply by reversing his surname and cutting out one letter 'b'. Unfortunately, from a modern perspective, this isn't the only stage name he used, as for a period of six years in the early 1900s he would apply stage makeup a wig and perform as Joad Heteb, an Egyptian conjurer, in an attempt to make himself appear more unique to audiences in London at the time.

Returning to his own persona, Selbit then went on to continue a successful career, including touring music halls and vaudeville theatres, St George's Hall, and even performing at a séance to which Sir Arthur Conan Doyle was invited, following which Doyle decided that Selbit was genuinely clairvoyant, apparently entirely missing the fact that Selbit was a magician.

This brings us back to January 1921, and the first public performance of his brand new trick, sawing a woman in half.

His assistant, Betty Barker, was placed into a large wooden box, as you can see in the picture at the start of this chapter, and secured with ropes around her wrists, ankles and neck, so that she would not be able to move out of the way of the saw-blade. The lid was sealed, and then the hard work began, as Selbit sawed the box in half. He then reopened the box, and released the woman from the ropes so that she could stand to show she was, after all, in one piece.

We can now pause for a moment, and consider where the skill, and therefore the credit in this performance really belongs. To do this, we need a working theory on the method of the trick, and to do this we need to figure out where the real trick is.

When you picture a magician sawing a woman into halves, you likely picture the woman in a box with her head stuck out one end, and her feet out the other end, thus providing a prover that she runs all the way through the box. It is also likely that you picture, after the box is sawn in half, that the halves are separated.

Neither of these elements is present in this first performance from Selbit, and so, once Barker was in the box and the lid closed, the only proof that the saw went through her was that she was tied in place when the lid was sealed. I personally haven't ever seen or read the secret of this version of the effect, but having just written chapters on Houdini and the Davenport Brothers with their spirit cabinet, I think that we can put the pieces together to figure out how the trick could have been accomplished.

I think we are left to conclude that in the performance of this version of the trick, P. T. Selbit's most difficult part of the trick was sawing a box in half, whereas Barker, if we have correctly surmised how the trick was done, would have to, in pitch darkness, remove the ropes restraining either her hands and neck, or the ones holding her feet, and then, once she had slipped the bonds to curl up safely out of the way of the saw, ensuring she was silent in her movements so that none of the spectators would hear her shuffling around inside the box. Then, once the saw was done, she had to return to her original position, including reattaching the ropes to her wrists, neck and ankle.

This, to my mind, shows clearly why, in my opinion, the magician at that point should be the one in the box, as that is where the magic is clearly happening.

There is also the question of why Selbit chose a woman to be in the box, when that was unnecessary. Did the fact that a mere three years before women had gained the right to vote in the UK, even though they had to be thirty and own a certain level of property, while men could then vote from 21 years of age with most property qualifications abolished, have anything to do with it?

I would have said, "No," but for the fact that Selbit approached Christabel Pankhurst, a woman's suffrage campaigner who had been imprisoned multiple times for her political protests, and had embarked on a hunger strike on one of those occasions, because he wanted her, specifically to be the woman inside the box, apparently offering her £20 per week (approximately £1252 today) if she would sign up for his full run of shows, which she refused, telling newspapers *The term at the Finsbury Empire is not the sort of work I am looking for.*

I may also be reading too much into this, and Selbit may not even have been considering the policical message it would send to have a campaigner for women's rights restrained in a box each night and sawn in half by a man live on stage, because he may have just seen someone with a lot of press attention who had recently placed adverts looking for employment.

In this way, he may have looked at it in the same way as the producers of 'I'm A Celebrity – Get Me Out Of Here' must have when they reached the decision to put the disgraced former Health Secretary Matt Hancock in their television show in 2022.

There is no question that Selbit knew the value of publicity, as each night following the performance he would have stagehands throw buckets of blood into the gutters outside the theatre's stage door, and even had nurses positioned in the theatre lobby.

The sawing in half trick quickly spread to other performers, and by the time Selbit wanted to tour his effect in America he found that another performer, Horace Goldin was already performing a version of his own, and had protected names of the trick which dealt with sawing people in half with the Vaudeville Managers' Protective Agency, meaning that for Selbit to perform the trick in America he had to call it 'The Divided Woman', which lost all of the impact of the name.

Selbit tried to sue Goldin for stealing his effect, while Goldin was also pursuing lawsuits against other magicians, but ultimately Selbit lost as it was decided that the two effects were too different for copyright laws to apply.

I think that Goldin's effect was not only significantly different to Selbit's, but also considerably better, both as a trick and as a piece of theatre.

In Goldin's version (which he received help to create from Thurston and a prop maker named Harry Jensen), the assistant's head and feet both stick out of the box and can be seen throughout the trick. After the sawing has taken place, large metal blades are slid into place where the saw had been, and then the two halves of the box are pulled apart, the head and legs still clearly visible.

Also, he first performed it, not with a female assistant, but with a bellboy getting sawn in half!

Magic Comes To Television

This, I think, is likely to be the riskiest chapter in the book
for me to write, in terms of risking upsetting people by
leaving out their favourite magicians. Up until this stage of
the book, I expect few people outside the magic
community to have heard of many magicians in this book
beyond Houdini. When we get into the subject of

television, however, I know that there will be people who feel that I have left out their favourite performer, whether that be Dynamo, The Great Soprendo, or many other names who have appeared on television through the years.

I could have written a whole book about television magic, and still not have managed to fit everybody in, which is why early in the book I pointed out that this is not a complete history of magic, therefore certainly not a complete history of television magic, and I have selected the magicians in this chapter based on their effect on television magic in general, and me in particular.

I think that I have covered my back as much as possible, though I don't know whether this will be enough to avoid a three-star review on Amazon from someone unhappy that I left out Chris Angel.

Mark Wilson – Appearing On The Small Screen

On the 1st of October 1960, just under nine years before Neil Armstrong walked on the moon, Mark Wilson took a giant leap for magicians.

Before that time, in 1955, Wilson had created a show called *'Time for Magic'*, sponsored by the Doctor Pepper Bottling Company, for a local television station in Dallas, Texas. It was in 1960, however, that Wilson appeared in front of the cameras in a show filmed in black and white, called *'Magic Land of Allakazam'*, featuring himself, with his wife, Nani Darnell, as his assistant, and Rebo the Clown played by Bev Bergeron.

The important development was that this show was videotaped rather than purely going out live, which allowed this to become the first nationally syndicated magic show. Suddenly people right across the United States, every Saturday morning for four years, could sit down and watch CBS-TV and see the same magic show airing.

Not only did Wilson take this huge step for magic, but he continued to perform throughout his life, even popping up as part of a trick on *'Penn and Teller's Fool Us'* in 2015.

Mark Wilson passed away in January 2021 at the age of ninety-one, but his influence on magic lives on, as I very often hear his book, *'Mark Wilson's Complete Course In Magic'*, which was released in 1975 and is still in print today, as one of the go-to books for a budding magician.

Tommy Cooper – Making Us Laugh!

There are some magicians who really divide opinion, and one of those is the great Tommy Cooper.

A large man, standing six foot four, with a red fez on the top, he was as much a comedian and prop-comic as he was a magician, and brought to the stage a huge sense of energy and fun.

His show was wonderfully fun, his catchphrase *"Just like that!"*, his madcap physical comedy, and his one-liners, often delivered with his trademark laugh at the end.

"I went to the doctors the other day and I said, "Have you got anything for wind?" So he gave me a kite."

"I want you to take a card. Now tear it into halves. Tear it into quarters. Tear it into eighths, and throw the pieces up in the air. Instant confetti!"

"One birthday my father bought me a bat. When I went to play with it, it flew away."

"I said, "It's serious, doctor, I've broken my arm in 20 places." He said, "Well stop going to those places."

I think it is fair to say, that when I am talking about Tommy Cooper dividing opinion, it wasn't over a question of this talent as a comedian or of his personality onstage, but on the question of whether he was actually a skilled magician.

Much of Cooper's humour in magic was derived from tricks seeming to go wrong, for example in his infamous *"Glass, bottle, bottle, glass"* routine, which you should really go and watch if you haven't done so yet.

This starts off simply as a classic trick known as 'Passe Passe' bottles, wherein a glass and a bottle are on a table, and each is covered with a tube, and when the tubes are lifted they have swapped places. In Cooper's routine, it immediately goes wrong when an extra bottle emerges from inside the wrong tube, which embarks on several minutes of growing speed, energy and laughter as more and more bottles start appearing until the table is full.

I have heard some people claim, that while he was a great entertainer, and was good at some tricks, he was actually not a very skilled magician, and many of his effects were created to show magic going wrong because he could not get the magic right. I have heard others claim that only a truly skilled magician could make the magic look as though it was going wrong.

For me, it matters very little, although I personally lean more towards the idea that he was a skilled magician. I just know that he performed in a hugely entertaining way, and created a persona far away from the usual 'magician as superman' persona which a lot of magicians cultivate as they work their miracles, to someone who was an underdog, who was always trying to make magic work, and who laughed when it went wrong, and seemed as surprised as the audience when it went right!

Tommy Cooper's death, equally, can split opinion, even within one's own heart. In 1984, live on television performing as part of a variety show at Her Majesty's Theatre, Tommy Cooper died from a coronary occlusion. He was on stage at the time, performing a routine involving a large cloak, when he leaned back on the curtain, and then collapsed to the floor.

Such was Cooper's onstage persona, it was assumed by most of the audience that this was part of his act, and they continued to laugh.

In some ways, this is an incredibly sad way for his life to end, with people laughing as he was dying. From another point of view, however, Tommy Cooper, who lived his life spreading laughter and joy from the stage, got to leave this world not with people crying around a hospital bed, but with the laughter he had created through his life ringing in his ears.

Fay Presto – Magic Up Close

Fay Presto is, without doubt, a magical legend, but one you may never have heard of outside the industry (although I hope that many of you will have done, and I sincerely hope that anyone in the industry will know who she is). She is the only person in this chapter who hasn't really had their own magic show or special on television, although she has appeared on television multiple times, and was the subject of 'Illusions of Grandeur', an episode of the BBC series '40 minutes', considered by many to be the best in the series, and her influence on magic is such that she couldn't be left out of the book.

Born in 1948, she started off her working life a little differently from any magician I have ever met, as a laboratory assistant at the Atomic Energy Research Establishment, which was a centre looking into the use of atomic power, and which was funded by the British Government to design and build nuclear reactors. She then moved into fashion for a brief period of time before moving into a job in engineering sales before, in her late thirties, she made one final major career switch into the world of show business.

The reason you may not have heard of her is that, although she has made a few television appearances, including on an episode of Paul Daniel's last magic series 'Secrets', playing herself as a cameo in Emmerdale, she was not pushing for a career in television, or performing in huge theatres.

Fay Presto is often credited, and rightfully so, in my opinion, for making one of the biggest shake-ups in magic since Robert-Houdin legitimised the art and brought magic to the parlours and theatres of the Victorian Era.

Have you ever been to a restaurant, or a wedding, or a party, and seen a magician working their way through the crowd or from table to table? This book started in my 'Overture' with a description of myself performing at just such an event.

This type of magic is generally referred to as 'close-up' magic, and Fay Presto is credited with creating this style of performance and she has been the resident magician at Langan's Brasserie in London's West End for more than twenty years.

The idea of close-up magic is so common in our profession these days, that the person who brought this version of our artform to the fore definitely deserves her place in any history of magic.

David Copperfield – A Magician and a Museum

I am, of course, going to begin to talk about David Copperfield by discussing his vanishing of the Statue of Liberty, the largest illusion ever staged in the world (confirmed by Guinness World Records) because it is such a classic of magic.

What I want to talk about most with Copperfield, however, is what he has done, and continues to do, for the whole topic of the history of magic. I must admit that when, after I announced that I was writing this book in July 2022, I saw Copperfield release a book on the same subject that October, I worried that the two books might be too similar, and with his involvement within the subject that I may have nothing to add. Fortunately, having listened to the first chapter on audible,[40] I realised that in the same way I enjoy watching two magicians perform the same trick for the different spins they put on the effect, my take in this book was going to be different enough that people will hopefully enjoy both.

For those of you unfamiliar with David Copperfield's work, who I can only assume are currently living under a rock on some remote island[41], perhaps the easiest way to show his prominence as a magician will be to list some of his awards and records.

---

[40] I am saving the rest as a treat for when I finish this book, as I did not want his fresh in my mind while I was writing. Even from that chapter, however, I feel safe strongly recommending the book.

[41] Not, presumably, one of the eleven, yes, eleven islands that Copperfield himself owns!

He has been named the 'Magician of the Century', and has
had a total, to date, of 38 Emmy Nominations with 21
wins, and a Living Legends Award from the Library of
Congress. He holds eleven Guinness World Records,
including 'Most Magic Shows Performed in a Year,
'Largest International Television Audience for a
Magician', and 'Most Tickets Sold Worldwide by a Solo
Entertainer'.

With his 1996 Broadway show, *'Dreams and Nightmares'*,
on which he collaborated with Frances Ford Coppola, he
got the Broadway record for most tickets sold in a week –
a record which he still holds today.

To put it simply, if there is anyone who can challenge
Houdini for the most famous magician of all time, then
that is David Copperfield.

In 1983, two years before I was born, Copperfield took a
leap into magic history when, in his fifth magic special for
CBS, he made the Statue of Liberty disappear, in front of
both a live and television audience, using no camera tricks
and no sneaky edits. As he explained in the documentary:

*"The Statue of Liberty, standing three hundred and five
feet high and weighing four hundred and fifty thousand
pounds… and I was going to make her disappear!"*

The live audience was sat on Liberty Island, two hundred
feet from the statue, with two towers just in front of them,
and the statue was lit up, with a helicopter flying overhead
as well. A curtain raises between the towers, is then

dropped, and the Statue of Liberty has vanished. It certainly is a step up from Houdini making an elephant disappear.

Then the curtain goes up, drops again, and the statue returns to its rightful place.

Even though people have had forty-years to figure out how the trick was achieved, and you can find no end of people who want to tell you the method (and I don't know whether Copperfield himself has ever confirmed the method, but I doubt it), they all miss the point of the effect if you ask me.

How he did it, the method, is so much less important than the effect itself. I found an article from 2021 where someone announces that *'We Finally Know How David Copperfield Made The Statue Of Liberty Disappear'*.

Imagine performing an effect that is so powerful that nearly forty years later there are still people writing articles trying to expose it, because the effect is still famous enough to draw people in.

Part of the reason for this is that the effect, not the method, is what is important here. Copperfield would have had a vast choice of statues or buildings which he could have 'vanished' in the special, but he chose the Statue of Liberty.

This wasn't a random choice, he knew that the symbolism of the statue and the freedom it represents to so many people would be something incredibly powerful to take away and then return in the effect.

You can tell, I think, that I have a lot of respect for Copperfield as a magician, but if anything I have even more respect for him as curator of magical history.

In Las Vegas, Copperfield houses a private museum, containing incredible artefacts from the history of magic, including, from what I have heard, much of Houdini's library and effects, the rifle that killed Chung Ling Soo, and even clocks made by Robert-Houdin.

I know about this museum only through stories of others, as the museum is not open to the public, and you have to be invited to visit, with Copperfield often leading tours of the museum himself. I hope one day, somehow, I will receive an invitation, as from what I have heard, for anyone interested in the background of our art form, this may be the most magical place in the world.

Sooty

I admit, there will be some serious-minded, and rather boring, people who think that Sooty has no place in a seriously considered history of magic. I don't think I would like to meet those people.

Sooty, the small yellow teddy bear with black ears and a black nose, certainly deserves his place here, as there is no other magical performer in the world who has a television career as long as Sooty has achieved.

Penn and Teller have had a television career lasting nearly twenty years so far, and David Copperfield has had over forty-five years since his first television appearance, and yet of these three magicians, only Teller was even born when Sooty first appeared on British television on the 16th of January 1955 (and even Teller would have been less than seven years old). Sooty last appeared on television in 2018, and as far as I know he has no plans to retire.

Sooty has had three magicians as his partners through the years, starting with Harry Corbett who discovered him, and the two worked together bringing magic to television screens and theatres until Harry retired and passed Sooty and the business on to his son, Matthew. Since 1998, Richard Cadell has been the magician working beside Sooty, and with him the little bear is in safe hands.

What is wonderful about Sooty, who is, and I hope I'm not going to upset anybody by revealing painful secrets here, a puppet, is the pure magic that he himself brings to the stage or screen. This is another wonderful example of the method being so much less important than the effect.

A lot of people know how a glove puppet works, and therefore how Sooty can move. The question of what brings Sooty to life, the effect of seeing this sweet, cheeky bear full of fun… that's just magic.

David Blaine

Although he may be better known today for his unusual stunts, such as being buried alive, or spending forty-four days in a plexiglass box suspended in the air on the South Bank of the River Thames in London, his initial impact on the world of magic came in 1997 when his first television special, *'Street Magic'* aired for the first time.

This was something new for television magic, although it has now become almost a standard style for filming magic shows. Unlike the likes of Paul Daniels or Tommy Cooper, who performed their shows on stages and in studios, Blaine's special took magic back to before the days when the likes of Robert-Houdin took it into grand theatres, and literally took his magic, with a camera crew, out onto the streets to perform for people.

This had the huge advantage of being much cheaper to film than a studio or theatre-based show, and yet it wouldn't have worked without Blaine and the production team really understanding what would make this new style of show work. It was all about the reactions.

It would not have been enough for Blaine to go out on the streets, and perform his effects to a small group of people while the camera focused on Blaine and the trick. Blaine knew, as every skilled close-up worker does, that if you find the right effect, and the right audience member, that the reactions can be absolutely huge. Screaming, gasps, the occasional expletive (beeped out on television, of course), all of these can happen. I even have one friend who frequently calls for me to be burned at the stake.

The point here is that when filming Blaine doing his magic in the streets, the camera crew knew to get these reactions on camera, and that these genuine reactions to close-up magic would give the audience much more of a feel of seeing the effect live than focussing on Blaine with the audience merely in the background. These genuine reactions told the audience that the magic was real, that it had the same effect live as it did on the screen.

In that one special alone, Blaine really set the stage for so much of what television magic would become moving forwards into the Twenty-First Century.

Derren Brown

If I talk about David Blaine's television shows setting the stage for television magic in the Twenty-First Century, then Derren Brown has had an impact which reaches out beyond television and into every level of magic, and certainly introduced me to one of my favourite styles of magic to perform.

We have spoken about the Victorian Séances, and the fraudulent mediums who used magic tricks to claim real psychic powers such as mindreading, or to pretend to communicate with the dead. This form of magic, commonly known as mentalism today, traces its roots back into that period, and many performers blur the lines between claiming that they are performing magic, and that they have real psychic powers.

One of the classic books to teach mentalism, by a performer named Tony Corinda, was released in the 1960s.

All of this is to say that the idea of magic of the mind was nothing new with Derren Brown, and even Paul Daniels had a section within some of his TV series called 'Extra Sensory Deception', in which he performed these types of effects.

It was, however, Brown's spin on this area of magic which captured the public imagination.

At the start of episodes of his *'Trick of the Mind'* series, he introduces viewers to the show by declaring that:

"This programme fuses magic, suggestion, psychology, misdirection and showmanship. I achieve all the results you'll see through a varied mixture of those techniques."

This, to me, is Derren Brown's spin on magic in a nutshell, in that he was clever enough at that point in time to list various aspects of the magician's art, with a leaning towards the techniques which others call mentalism, and make them clear to an audience, while allowing the audience members to then focus on certain words.

I know sometimes I am at a show or event and the first reaction a lot of adults have to seeing a magician (bearing in mind I am usually beside a sign saying 'Magic and Mindreading' and dressed in fairly formal attire, with shirt, waistcoat and, depending on the temperature, a tailcoat[42]), is that it must be fun for children.

---

[42] My current show shirts, waistcoat and most of my tailcoats are thanks to Rob and Jill at SteampunkDotGlobal, while my other tailcoat (which you will see in my

Let me be clear here. Magic is fun for children, and at a lot of events I do magic for children. However, magic is also fun and interesting for adults. There does, however, seem to be an odd mental block with a certain percentage of the population that, until you show them an entertaining effect, makes them think that magic is for children only, or not for them, at least[43].

The methods which Brown lists here are, to my mind, different aspects that most good magicians consider when working on a magic trick.

Go back to the simple card trick which we learnt earlier on from 'The Discoverie of Witchcraft'. Remember how we used repeated shuffles to *suggest* that the cards were entirely random. We then looked away when they all looked at the card to *misdirect* the audience from the moment the trick has occurred. We knew from understanding some basic *psychology* of a participant that they may try to lie, or forget the card, and so we showed it to everyone. Finally, it was our *'showmanship'* which allowed us to sell the moment of reveal as our finger locates the card.

'Greg Chapman's Magic Show' videos was made by the wonderful Lurcher Gallery.

[43] One thing that I find both ego-boosting and heart-breaking in equal measure, is the number of times people say to me *"I don't like magicians, but I really enjoyed your show."* What these people, I think, mean, is that they have seen a magician they didn't enjoy, and lumped all magicians into that category, so I must be the exception. I flatter myself that I am a good magician, and I know how to bring magic to an effect, but I wish these people would take away the idea that they actually like magic performed well, and not that I am some exception to the rule.

You can see how all of these factors have been used by every one of the magicians we have talked about throughout this book, they just haven't listed them (and nor, for the record, do I, unless I am discussing elements of the subject).

This is not to say that Derren Brown's knowledge of succession and psychology are not profound. I think it is the depth of his skill and experience that not only made him the name he is today, but also suggested that list at the beginning of the episodes. I am speculating here, but I would guess that he knew full well that by making that list, people's minds would latch on to words like 'pyschology', 'misdirection', and 'suggestion', and not focus on the word magic.

This has the dual effect of distracting the people who think 'magicians are for children' away from the word magic, because psychology and suggestion sound much more 'grown up', while also being open and honest about using magic in a way that people quickly forget, so that they are not looking for magical methods behind some of his effects, even if they are there.

In this way, Derren Brown may have made the biggest impact away from 'magic is for children' of any magician I know, and I have been asked many times when adults are booking performances for their friends whether I do the "Derren Brown mindreading stuff". The great thing about this is it allows me, and I imagine other magicians like me to then take a gig and perform some mentalism, while allowing for a slide then into many different styles of magic.

Derren Brown has continued to push the boundaries where magic meets psychology, which has led to some truly ground breaking specials, and is doubtless one of the best magical minds today. I have a copy of two books he wrote before he was famous, with magicians in mind (which nowadays change hands for a lot of money, and require a certain level of knowledge of magic to read), which really show the mind and thought processes behind what he does.

Penn & Teller Fool Us

I could write a book, or several, about Penn & Teller. I have listened for the past eleven years to Penn's podcast, 'Penn's Sunday School', and heard him tell stories of everything from the early days of Penn and Teller, right through to working on their current shows and effects, and I suggest that that podcast is the place to go to hear those stories, especially if you find the episode with Teller on as well.

For those of you who don't know Penn & Teller, they are a magical duo who have been performing together since the 1970s, starting with performances at Minnesota Renaissance Festival on August 19, 1975, and are currently the longest running headline act at the same theatre in Las Vegas.

Penn, the taller, louder one of the two, started out as a juggler, and does all of the talking in the Penn & Teller show, while Teller performs silently, with a wonderfully expressive face, and magical skills that may possibly be the very best in the world today. Both are kind and generous with their time for their fans.

I have always made an effort to meet people after a show, which started for me when touring schools in Italy (when heading to the door to say, "Goodbye," to the children would stop them rushing the stage!), and it has stuck since then and I enjoy it. I, however, might have up to a couple of hundred people to meet, with Penn & Teller that can be thousands. When I got to see them at the Hammersmith Apollo in 2017, which has over three and a half thousand seats, they stood outside and chatted with people, and took photographs, until they had seen everyone who wanted to meet them, long after we had taken our photos and left!

A top piece of advice for stage magicians, if you would enjoy it, is to meet your audiences. I have learned so much about my shows that way, including that some audiences are very quiet during a show because they have been concentrating so much, and without meeting them after the show you could easily mistake the quiet for an audience not enjoying it.

In order to stop the section on Penn & Teller from doubling the size of the book (because if I do it for them, I'll want to add more to all of the other chapters as well, and this book will never be finished), I'm going to talk about their most recent television show, and one which I think may be the perfect way to show stage magic on television, 'Penn & Teller Fool Us'.

The concept of the show is very simple. The host (in the first two seasons it was Jonathan Ross, and from then on Alison Hannigan) introduces a number of magicians, who each come onto the stage to perform a magic routine.

These could be relatively unknown performers, or more established names such as Mac King, Morgan and West, John Archer, or Helen Coghlan[44].

Each magician performs a trick, and the supposed goal is to come up with a method which can fool Penn & Teller, who have a few minutes after each trick to try to talk together about how the trick was done, and then Penn will, through coded language, hint at how they think the trick was achieved. Most magicians will accept it quickly if they think Penn & Teller are right about how the trick was achieved, and there is a magical expert listening in who can confirm whether or not they have it correct (this was the great Johnny Thompson until he sadly passed away in early 2019).

If they 'win' they get to perform a routine at the Penn & Teller theatre alongside one of the Penn & Teller shows, although some of the acts on there have realised that in order to really 'win' the show you may not have to fool Penn & Teller at all.

---

[44] As I mentioned Helen Coghlan, I want to go back to a point which I brought up in the chapter on Victorian Magicians. I mentioned that there have, throughout the history of magic, been very few female magicians.

There is light at the end of the tunnel and optimistic points on the horizon, as shown in 'Penn and Teller: Fool Us', of about forty-one magicians competing in the first series, I counted only three female magicians, which is once again around seven per cent.

By the time we get to the eighth series, of sixty-one magicians competing, twelve are female, bringing it up to nearly twenty per cent! This isn't an equal number, obviously, but it really shows a move in the right direction!

By far, the breakout performer from the first few series, if not from all the series so far, was Piff the Magic Dragon, who did not fool them on his first appearance. Proving one of the messages which has run through this book, however, that didn't really matter. In fact, Piff showed how little it meant to him as, instead of nervously talking with the host and shooting glances over at Penn & Teller while they were deliberating over the method, he nonchalantly began to eat a banana.

He knew that the real winner of the show was going to be someone who got onstage and gave an entertaining performance that the audience in the theatre, the audience at home, and Penn & Teller all enjoyed, and as soon as they suggested they knew how it was done he accepted it with no push back.

This is why, for me, this is very close to the perfect solution to a stage magic show. Unlike something like 'Britain's Got Talent', or other competition-based shows, you are not going to be 'buzzed', put down, or badly edited by the judges and production company. The only judgement is on whether you have fooled Penn & Teller, which is an objective point, not a matter of opinion.

From that point of view it is more of a magical showcase show, allowing audiences to see a lot of different magicians performing. The element of competition is, conversely, exactly what makes the format work. In a world where camera tricks and editing tricks can be used, what better way to prove that none of the acts on the show can use anything like that, because it is a competition with rules, and you know that whatever effect they have performed, it has been performed with two of the greatest magicians in the world today watching very closely.

Katherine Mills

One final name to mention before we reach the end of the chapter is Katherine Mills.

Mills became interested in magic after the David Blaine special came out, before going on to study social psychology at university.

Her step into television came in 2012, when she joined James Went, Fergus Flannigan and John Archer as the magicians on a CBBC television series 'Help! My Supply Teacher is Magic'. This series involved the magicians going undercover into schools, and applying a magical twist to the lessons. The show proved popular enough, and was good enough quality, to receive a Children's BAFTA in 2013 for the best entertainment show.

Having shared the screen with her fellow magicians in that series, on the 2nd October 2014, fifty-four years and a day after Mark Wilson became the first magician with a nationally syndicated television show, Katherine Mills became the first female magician to front her own prime time television show in the UK, with 'Katherine Mills: Mind Games', a four episode magic series made with Objective productions, the company who were also behind the series 'Killer Magic' and 'Help! My Supply Teacher's Magic'.

While all of the magicians in this chapter have served to make the first six decades of television magic a widely varied spectacle, there is one magician from the television era who stands head and shoulders above the rest in their impact on my magic career, and the career of many magicians I know…

The Paul Daniels Magic Kit

It seems strange to me, as I'm sure it will for many in my generation and above in the UK, that a lot of people younger than me (and it is less than five years younger than me that the cut-off occurs) will not know the name Paul Daniels any more than they will have recognised the name Robert-Houdin.[45] In my shows I often deliberately mention the 'Paul Daniel's Magic Kit' to see a wave of nostalgia pass across the faces of people who were born before approximately 1989 and to see absolutely no recognition from those people younger than that (although since his wife and assistant, 'the lovely Debbie Mcgee' made it to the final of 'Strictly Come Dancing' in 2017, and won the Christmas special of the same show in 2019, a few more younger people seem to recognise the name). So, a short introduction may be necessary.

---

[45] Although I hope that most of my brothers and sisters in magic will have recognised both names.

For many years, Paul Daniels was the most prominent magician on British television and can almost certainly be credited with starting an interest in magic for many magicians performing in the UK today.

My earliest memory of watching magic on television is sitting down as a child and watching 'The Paul Daniels Magic Show'.

There was one effect performed by Paul[46] that has stayed vividly in my memory for at least thirty years. I have never seen a video of this routine (and I have searched for it a lot), but I can close my eyes now and still vividly recall him presenting this trick. I now have a version of this trick (although I wouldn't repeat Paul's presentation), but even knowing how the trick is done, and performing a version of it myself, has not diminished the 'magic' of seeing the trick for the first time.

Working entirely from a childhood memory[47] from when I was less than ten years old, as the Paul Daniels Magic Show ran from 1979 – 1994, ending less than two weeks ahead of my ninth birthday, I will describe the effect.

I don't know if he introduced this particular trick with his classic catchphrase, "You'll like this. Not a lot, but you'll

---

[46] I have decided to use 'Paul' in this chapter instead of referring to him as 'Mr Daniels' or repeatedly saying 'Paul Daniels'. The reason for this is that 'Paul' is how he asked his participants in his effects to refer to him, often saying things like: "Say 'Yes, Paul".

[47] As sadly the 'Paul Daniel's Magic Show' is available neither on DVD, streaming, or even VHS, as I would really like to see this again.

like it", which he apparently happened upon one night in a performance in Yorkshire while dealing with a heckler.

On that particular night, a man in the audience shouted out to Paul that he didn't like his suit, to which Paul responded:

"That's a shame. Cos I like yours. Not a lot, but I like it."

As the consummate professional that he was, Paul knew the value of a callback and kept referring to the line throughout the remainder of the show, and he never looked back. In fact, in his autobiography, he says that when the catchphrase was entered into the 'Dictionary of Colloquialisms and Common Language', it was better than getting a chance to perform at the Royal Variety Show!

Back to young Greg sat in front of the television set in the early 1990s, with Paul and a participant onstage, delivering what I would consider a masterclass in taking a relatively classic trick, which would take about 30 seconds to perform, and turning it into a wonderful story-driven effect. I think, at some level, this single effect had a huge influence on me when I began to learn magic, and that is why I often approach my tricks from a 'story first' point of view.

Paul began to explain the legend of King Arthur and the sword Excalibur and how whoever held Excalibur in their hand would win any battle and could not be harmed. On King Arthur's death, the sword was thrown into a lake to be returned to the Lady of the Lake.

He then went on to tell that near Tintagel Castle in Cornwall, which some people consider to be the legendary birthplace of King Arthur, they sell small letter-opener-sized replicas of Excalibur, which they claim are made from the real sword after it had been found and melted down, and therefore would contain the same power of invulnerability as the full sword.

Paul took out one of these small souvenir swords and handed it to the volunteer, and then brought out a small wooden guillotine with a hole just big enough for one finger to go through. He removed the blade and showed that it was solid, save for a hole in the centre, which lined up with the hole in the guillotine.

The participant held the sword in one hand, and placed the index finger of the other hand through the hole in the guillotine, after which, following a bit of build-up, Paul pushed the blade down through the finger, leaving the finger completely intact. More than that, as Paul then disassembled the guillotine, it was seen that the participant's finger was really poking through the hole in the centre of the solid blade.

In recent years, I have seen this same trick performed on a number of occasions. I have seen one brilliant version, performed by the great Mr Alexander in his travelling show, which turns the trick into a miniature play involving a whole group of children as participants playing different roles in a real tour-de-force of building up to a trick.

On the contrary, I have seen a lot of lesser versions where there is little build to the trick, and it is over before the audience has even had a chance to get interested.

While it would be many years later that a bag and an egg, in a school hall in Italy, would drive me down a magical path, when I did get into magic in a big way I began to appreciate Paul Daniels more and more.

Paul was a true master at taking the quickest of tricks and creating a truly theatrical effect from them. I know a number of magicians who do this very well, and I hope that I can count myself in this number (and, modesty aside, one of the comments which I often get, and I always take as the highest compliment, is when people tell me I am an entertainer or a storyteller as much as a magician[48]).

What sets Paul Daniels apart from anyone else I can think of, is the sheer quantity of material which he produced. I generally add a couple of hours of new material into my act each year, between new shows and new effects for my close-up performances. Over a period of fifteen years, Paul created 128 episodes and 21 specials, which is an incredible amount of new material and tricks which he had to learn, practice, figure out a presentation for, work out how the cameras should be positioned, and then actually perform in front of the TV cameras and a live audience.

---

[48] Feel free to ignore this footnote if you think it is bad form to share praise of myself in this book, but one of the proudest moments in my magical career was a day I performed for a party of adults in Wargrave, about three years after his sad passing in 2016. One of the guests had seen him perform a number of times, and told me that Paul often referred to himself as a 'funjourer', and that I should do the same. I don't, as I couldn't compare myself to Paul Daniels, but it meant a lot.

Even with the assistance of producers, directors, and magical minds like Ali Bongo, that is an incredible amount of effects to create every year over that time. He has spoken about the fact that a lot of his time, when not performing or rehearsing, was spent reading through magic books (something which we share), and I am very proud to have, in my own magical library, a number of books from Paul's own magical library.

There is another connection between myself and Paul Daniels to do with books, which I really think speaks to the man behind the magic.

One of the few things I look back and feel I missed out on is that I never got to see Paul Daniels perform live, and I never got to meet him in person, although we did once share a couple of messages on Twitter.

When, a little over a decade ago, I wrote a short history book containing a number of stories from the history of England, I tried messaging a few celebrities on Twitter to see if any of them could share about the book for me.

I got very few replies (as you would assume – they must get many, many requests every day), but one of the few I got was from Paul. His message told me that not only was he was happy to share, but he had just bought the Kindle edition of the book. Paul Daniels was, in fact, the first person ever to buy my first book on Kindle.

That would have been kind enough as it was, but then, a couple of weeks later, he messaged me again just to say that he had read the book and enjoyed it.

That was the entirety of my personal interaction with him, and yet that he had taken the time, for a fan, to buy and read the book, and even to then message me afterwards, is for me a real testament to his personality, and is the reason that I try to respond with a personal message to anybody who messages me who knows me only through seeing me perform.

He is truly one of the great magical performers, and I strongly recommend you try to find some of his work to watch if you can (I have already mentioned his cup and ball routine in an earlier chapter). Paul Daniels came from humble beginnings, born in 1938 in his grandmother's house in South Bank, an industrial town in the north-east of England, but grew to become true magical royalty.

You will notice, however, that this chapter is not titled 'Paul Daniels' or 'The Paul Daniels Magic Show', but is instead titled 'The Paul Daniels Magic Kit'.

I had one of these magic kits as a child, and although the one I owned as a child has been lost somewhere in the dim and distant past, I do own a couple of sets now which I have obtained over the years on eBay, including the one I am pictured with onstage at the start of this chapter, and it is these magic sets which a lot of magicians who were young in the era of Paul Daniels credit with starting their fascination with magic.

Here is one of the reasons why I have deliberately included a couple of old magic tricks in this book and why, at a show, if it feels right and I have the right person in front of me, I will teach them a trick.

To watch a magician on television is one thing for a child, where you can be entertained and impressed by the magic, but I think that if that had been all there was, it would not have inspired as many magicians as it has.

It was, I think, the fact that you could see this magician on television and then get a box with his face on the front and a booklet he had written inside to start to learn your first magic tricks and to allow you to share that experience of entertaining and fooling someone with a little piece of magic of your own.

The really good thing about the 'Paul Daniel's Magic Kit' (and although I am referring to it as though it is one kit, there are many different versions of the kit from various years) is that a lot of the tricks in there will teach you basic principles of magic, but also that many of the tricks are real 'foolers' if performed well. In fact, I have adapted a few of the tricks from the kits I have bought from eBay and actually perform them in my shows today, particularly enjoying being able to spread bafflement and happiness to adults with tricks I could have had in my magic set when I was less than ten years old.

Learning magic from Paul Daniels wasn't limited to boxes filled with various effects either. One of my more recent Paul Daniels related acquisitions is a copy of his 'magic wallet', a plastic wallet containing ten different packet tricks.[49]

---

[49] A packet trick, in the simplest terms, is a trick which uses only a small number of cards rather than the complete deck. These can be useful to a magician as you can slip several different packet tricks into a pocket and if you are doing a roaming close-up performance moving through lots of people, pocket space is at a premium.

Once again, with practice, a little modification[50], and the correct presentation, these can all be great effects. I am trying to decide at the moment whether I will create fresh versions and perform them as standalone effects, or in some way, build a routine specifically around the fact that these are tricks from this Paul Daniels set and talk about him a little.[51]

To give you an idea of just how many magicians from my generation started with one of his magic sets, in an interview with 'The Magician's Podcast[52]' back in 2015, the host, magician Richard Young, started the interview by saying:

"First of all, you're the only magician who is going to appear on this podcast who didn't start with a 'Paul Daniels Magic Kit.'"

In the later years of his life, Paul even set up a YouTube channel, which at the time of writing is still active, containing some behind-the-scenes videos of his tour at the time, some wonderful advice for magicians, and even an 'Unboxing video'!

In my mind, one of the most important things that Paul Daniels can teach, and which made his magic series what it

---

[50] This is not because there is anything wrong with these tricks, but I have never had a trick which I didn't in some way have to modify to work slightly better. In fact, Paul himself has spoken about how good it is when starting work on a new trick to 'pull it apart' and then see how it can be improved.

[51] Can you tell he is one of the magicians I most enjoy talking about?

[52] If you are starting out in magic, this is a very interesting podcast to listen to with so many top magicians being interviewed.

was, is that he took the time to learn various different aspects of the creation of television shows. He understood camera positions and angles, and he understood editing well enough to have clear rules when it came to the edits in his television shows.

One of the key elements of this was to have a 'point of no return', the moment in a magic trick performed on television, beyond which the camera could not cut, either away from the action or even just in a change of camera angle, because you needed that continuous shot to avoid the possibility that the audience would believe that you are using camera edits in order to accomplish the trick[53].

As you may be able to tell, both from this chapter and because I have decided to write this book about the history of magic, that line running through time from the past, through the present, and onto the future is one that means a lot to me, in my life, in my interests, and my performances. That is why one of the greatest treasures in my magic collection is one magic trick which was bought for me a few years ago by Felicity as a birthday present.

The trick's apparatus takes the form of a wooden cut-out of a bellhop and is a lovely effect for having one spectator pick a card and then a second spectator (with the help of

---

[53] There is an argument against this nowadays given modern technology. Now that streaming allows people to rewatch a trick immediately and to rewatch it in slow motion, I have heard the point of view put forward that camera edits should be allowed in order to make the magic on television create the same effect on the viewer at home as on somebody watching it live. This is more a question of editing choices than 'camera tricks', however, I am still yet to be convinced by this particular take on the subject.

the bellhop) chooses the same card from the deck. This trick mostly lives at home with my collection, but on occasion comes out for a performance here or there.

The part that makes this trick so important to me is that it is one from Paul Daniels' own collection. It has a certificate of authenticity signed by him and even typewritten notes from him with his instructions and thoughts on the performance of the trick. What makes it extra special is that the first time my father saw me perform the trick live, he came over to me at the end to tell me that he remembered Paul Daniels performing this very trick, with this very prop, on The Paul Daniels Magic Show' nearly thirty years earlier.

Cosmic Xposure

The Future of Magic

We have now taken magic from its first recorded origins right up, almost to the current day, and our little journey through magic is fast approaching the final curtain.

As I look back on all I have written, the question in my mind is about the future of magic, what it looks like, and does magic have a future?

The last part of that sentence may seem a little bit extreme, a little melodramatic, but it is a question I have seriously heard discussed. As we move forward into a world where CGI continues to grow, where 'deep fakes' and AI are creeping in, and where holograms look to be something of the future, then does magic have a future? If, in thirty years' time, I can have a hologram of an elephant on stage, then where would the mystery be in taking after Houdini and having the elephant disappear?[54]

I think the simple answer to this is that magicians will change with the times. There were people when magic went to television who I am sure would have thought similar things, but it never happened. As magicians, part of our job is to not only perform a magic trick but also to include 'provers', to add elements to the trick to ensure that people can see this isn't some simple piece of technology being used... even if there is some form of technology being used.

I mentioned earlier that saying 'this is a perfectly ordinary deck of cards' is a mistake, but when I take out a deck of cards to perform a trick, I will generally play with the cards first, fanning them in my hands so that people can see they are all different. This is a prover.

When Victorian Magicians would make a girl levitate into the air, they would then get a large metal hoop and pass it over the girl to prove that she could not possibly be held up with wires. Let me ask you to imagine, however, that a magician just wanted to do things the easy way and have the girl on wires, wouldn't the real trick, the real 'prover', be to figure out how a solid metal hoop could pass through those wires, while you were already looking for solutions in all the wrong places? That would be a great prover.

---

[54] I am, of course, talking in hyperbole here. I would absolutely be against an elephant being brought into a theatre and used in a magic trick. Although we are talking about a holographic elephant. Although if the audience knew it was a holographic elephant, then there is no magic, so, just remember the elephant, whether it is holographic or real, is in either case a hyperbolic elephant.

Magic will not die out, not in our lifetimes, and I am quite sure it will never fade away as long as there are sentient creatures in the universe.

I remember when smartphones were suddenly everywhere, and people were afraid that the capabilities of a smartphone would make people think that they were being used for all sorts of tricks, so magicians had to take that possibility off the table or put it out of people's minds when they present the effect.

Magicians, however, as a group, are far cleverer than that. A lot of close-up magicians now look at a smartphone the way magicians look at a deck of cards, a coin, a banknote, or any other commonplace object. A smartphone is something which we are all so familiar with that if a magician can take yours and make it do something it could never possibly do, like folding it in half or pushing a nail through the centre of it,[55] then it is every bit as powerful, if not more so, than a magician making a coin pass through the bottom of a glass.

There will also be new famous magicians in the future, and there may be someone sitting on a computer in a biodome on Jupiter in a hundred-years time writing their own history of magic. Anyone's name could end up in the book as the greatest magician of the 21st Century.

Maybe even yours.

---

[55] Do not try either of these things unless you know and are confident with a proven magical method for the trick!

Cosmic Xposure

Curtain Call

It is nearly time for the curtain to come down on our journey together through the history of magic, so this is a good opportunity to see how far we've come... and to look at how, in some ways, we have stayed in the same place.

As I write this epilogue (a Friday in June, as I have taken a few days off shows to finish this book), I know that tomorrow morning I must select my tricks, check that they are all correctly set up, and load up my van for this weekend's shows. I know that among the tricks which will be going into my magic box for the show will be a cup and a small, crocheted ball. I will almost certainly perform this trick, and although I have my own words and my own routine for the effect, the trick itself is essentially the same as that which was performed by the jugglers of Ancient

Roman times, a clear thread running through the history of magic, and seen in the hands of so many performers through the years.

This is why I have had an interest in the history of magic ever since I first started to seriously study the art form. I did not invent magic, nor did anyone alive today. We don't even know who did, and yet every time I walk onstage, or have someone come over to see my magic at an event, or I approach a group at a walkaround performance, I remind myself that what I am about to do can be traced back through history, and I am proud to be part of a tradition and culture which, at its core and at its best, has been about entertaining people, about bringing a special connection between people, and, just for a moment, about taking people out of the logic of the real world, even just for a moment, to a place where everything isn't quite as real as it seems.

I am glad that magic has grown from humble beginnings to the point where top-name magicians can sell out large theatre tours in minutes if they so choose, and less famous magicians like myself can tour smaller theatres, close-up shows and private parties to bring magic into more and more people's lives. I am also glad to see that over the past few decades, the stereotype of a magician as being male with a female assistant has begun to fade away, with more and more wonderful female magicians coming to prominence.

I hope that you have enjoyed my book. Much like my shows, I hope that it has brought you moments of joy, moments of interest and perhaps taught you something along the way. I have hopes that it may inspire some of you to learn even a single magic trick which you can then perform to make people smile. I hope that this book may inspire a young magician to dig deeper into the past to learn more about the history of the magic which we get to share and perhaps to learn more about some of the infamous and slightly less famous magicians from the past.

I am by no means a famous magician, which means at this point, I would like to ask you all a couple of favours to help me achieve my hopes with this book. If you have enjoyed the book,[56] then please take the time to leave a review on Amazon or any other site where you can leave a review for it – this is really the single most important thing you can do to help a writer's work get found these days. Also, please tell a friend who you think might be interested in the book.

Above all, if you see me at a show, do come over, when I am not performing, to have a chat with me about the history of magic – as you may be able to tell, it is one of my favourite subjects, and it is always a pleasure to talk to people about it.

If you are a member of a group which would be interested in booking a talk on the history of magic with some magic thrown in, feel free to send me an email.

---

[56] If you have made it all the way to this stage of the book, I certainly hope that you have enjoyed it!

For now, though, I have nearly reached the ending of the book, the ending of this show.

I take my final bow and take a step backwards from the footlights to allow the curtain to come down for the final time. I pause for a moment, as I know on the other side of the cloth, the lights will start to come back on fully in the auditorium, and you, the audience, will move from silence to a hum of noise as you all begin to discuss what you have seen.

In the real world, I would then begin to make my way through the hidden corridors in the backstage areas of the theatre, hoping to reach the foyer before the first members of the audience (a far easier job a few years ago before I had to walk with a stick!).

In print, I can't do this, although I look forward to seeing your reviews, talking to you at shows, and getting to share my magic with you live at some point in the future.

For now, I wish you all the most magical of lives.

Yours in magic,

Greg

Greg Chapman
Magician and Magic Fan
www.gregchapman.net
greg.chapman@gregandfelicity.com

Special Thanks

Felicity – Thank you for all you do for me. For putting up with the hours of me scrabbling through books and for the piles of books scattered around. Most importantly, for being the greatest magic in my life.

Cosmic Xposure – The majority of the photographs of me throughout this book were taken by Suezan and Barry of Cosmic Xposure (you will see their logos on the photos). They are great event and show photographers, and I really can't thank them enough for allowing me to use their photos in this book.

Jackie – For proofreading the book. Needless to say, any mistakes remain my own.

To Mum and Dad – For my first 'Paul Daniels Magic Kit'.

Rupert – For introducing me to magic in performance, for a decade of 'on the job' training on tour in Italy, and for allowing me to read from your magic collection.

To Mr Alexander – For treating a young performer, new to the circuit, many years ago, like an equal, and for our friendship.

My personal, deep and sincere thanks to all of these people who supported this book on Ko-Fi, and let me know each word I wrote, every time I deleted and rewrote a whole page, and every time I spent hours trawling through books to confirm some half-remembered fact, that there were people out there interested in and waiting for this book.

Mike Lush
The Judge Mentalist
Barbara Llewellyn
Winging It Travel Podcast
Matt Donnelly - The Mind Noodler
Gurdybird
Gregory O'Regan
Steve Wardhaugh
Huxley
Maggie Currie
Kathryn Ward
Maureen Sullivan
Helen Canning
Tyler Shorter
Robert Paulseni
Jem Duducu
Richard Heath
Lurcher Gallery
Robby Measday
Jess, Josh & Hendrix
Therese Prior
Mark Dunsford
Jake Blankenship
Robert Flute
Adrian Pryke
Lisa Robinson
Jeanette Macklin
Steve Love

Further Reading

Here are some books I would recommend, some for those who want to read more about the history of magic and others for those of you interested in learning a little magic of your own (until I get around to getting a magic book out myself someday!).

Magic History

Paul Daniels and the Story of Magic - John Fisher

A Magician Among the Spirits - Harry Houdini

The Memoirs of Robert-Houdin – Jean-Eugène Robert-Houdin

Paul Daniels - My Magic Life: The Autobiography – Paul Daniels

Happy – Derren Brown (For more about Stoic Philosophy)

Victorian Magic – Geoffrey Lamb

Escape!: The Story of the Great Houdini by Sid Fleischman

David Copperfield's History of Magic - David Copperfield

Hiding The Elephant - Jim Steinmeyer

Learning Magic

The Royal Road To Card Magic – Jean Hugard

Paul Daniels' Magic Book – Paul Daniels

Tricks Of The Mind - Derren Brown

Modern Coin Magic - J. B. Bobo

Classic Secrets of Magic - Bruce Elliott

Mark Wilson's Complete Course In Magic – Mark Wilson

Printed in Great Britain
by Amazon

40625964R00106